W9-BJU-309

DATE DUE

Cocaine

Other books in the History of Drugs series:

Cocaine

EDITED BY EMMA CARLSON BERNE

Bruce Glassman, *Vice President*

Bonnie Szumski, *Publisher*

Helen Cothran, *Managing Editor*

GREENHAVEN PRESS

An imprint of Thomson Gale, a part of The Thomson Corporation

THOMSON
━━━★━━━ ™
GALE

Detroit • New York • San Francisco • San Diego • New Haven, Conn.
Waterville, Maine • London • Munich

LIBRARY OF CONGRESS CATALOGING-IN-PUBLICATION DATA

Cocaine / Emma Carlson Berne, book editor.
   p. cm. — (The history of drugs)
Includes bibliographical references and index.
ISBN 0-7377-1955-9 (lib. : alk. paper)
   1. Cocaine habit—History. 2. Cocaine—History. 3. Crack (Drug)—History.
4. Coca—History. I. Berne, Emma Carlson. II. Series.
HV5810.C618 2006
616.86'47—dc22
                                         2005046353

Printed in the United States of America

CONTENTS

drug cocaine. One important medical leader recounts his positive personal experiences with the narcotic.

CHAPTER TWO: EXPLORING COCAINE IN THE 1960S, '70S, AND '80S

CHAPTER THREE: CRACK: THE OTHER COCAINE

CHAPTER FOUR: CURRENT ISSUES AND CONTROVERSIES

Drugs are chemical compounds that affect the functioning of the body and the mind. While the U.S. Food, Drug, and Cosmetic Act defines drugs as substances intended for use in the cure, mitigation, treatment, or prevention of disease, humans have long used drugs for recreational and religious purposes as well as for healing and medicinal purposes. Depending on context, then, the term *drug* provokes various reactions. In recent years, the widespread problem of substance abuse and addiction has often given the word *drug* a negative connotation. Nevertheless, drugs have made possible a revolution in the way modern doctors treat disease. The tension arising from the myriad ways drugs can be used is what makes their history so fascinating. Positioned at the intersection of science, anthropology, religion, therapy, sociology, and cultural studies, the history of drugs offers intriguing insights on medical discovery, cultural conflict, and the bright and dark sides of human innovation and experimentation.

Drugs are commonly grouped in three broad categories: over-the-counter drugs, prescription drugs, and illegal drugs. A historical examination of drugs, however, invites students and interested readers to observe the development of these categories and to see how arbitrary and changeable they can be. A particular drug's status is often the result of social and political forces that may not necessarily reflect its medicinal effects or its potential dangers. Marijuana, for example, is currently classified as an illegal Schedule I substance by the U.S. federal government, defining it as a drug with a high potential for abuse and no currently accepted medical use. Yet in 1850 it was included in the U.S. *Pharmacopoeia* as a medicine, and solutions and tinctures containing cannabis were frequently prescribed for relieving pain and inducing sleep. In the 1930s, after smokable marijuana had gained notoriety as a recreational intoxicant, the Federal Bureau of Narcotics launched a misinformation campaign against the drug, claiming that it commonly induced insanity and murderous violence. While today's medical experts no longer make such claims about marijuana, they continue to disagree about the drug's long-term effects and medicinal potential. Most interestingly, several states have passed medical marijuana initiatives, which allow seriously ill patients compassionate access to the drug under state law—although these patients can still be prosecuted for marijuana use under federal law. Marijuana's illegal status, then, is not as fixed or final as the federal government's current schedule might suggest. Examining marijuana from a historical perspective offers readers the chance to develop a more sophisticated and critically informed view of a controversial and politically charged subject. It also encourages students to learn about aspects of medicine, history, and culture that may receive scant attention in textbooks.

Each book in Greenhaven's The History of Drugs series chronicles a particular substance or group of related drugs—discussing the appearance and earliest use of the drug in initial chapters and more recent and contemporary controversies in later chapters. With the incorporation of both primary and secondary sources written by physicians, anthropologists, psychologists, historians, social analysts, and lawmakers, each anthology provides an engaging panoramic view of its subject. Selections include a variety of readings, including book excerpts, government documents, newspaper editorials, academic articles, and personal narratives. The editors of each volume aim to include accounts of notable incidents, ideas, subcultures, or individuals connected with the drug's history as well as perspectives on the effects, benefits, dangers, and legal status of the drug.

Every volume in the series includes an introductory essay that presents a broad overview of the drug in question. The annotated table of contents and comprehensive index help readers quickly locate material of interest. Each selection is prefaced by a summary of the article that also provides any necessary historical context and biographical information on the author. Several other research aids are also present, including excerpts of supplementary material, a time line of relevant historical events, the U.S. government's current drug schedule, a fact sheet detailing drug effects, and a bibliography of helpful sources.

Greenhaven Press's The History of Drugs series gives readers a unique and informative introduction to an often-ignored facet of scientific and cultural history. The contents of each anthology provide a valuable resource for general readers as well as for students interested in medicine, political science, philosophy, and social studies.

Testimonies from people who have used cocaine tend to emphasize the drug's sometimes terrifying, sometimes exhilarating strength. Users of the drug sometimes refer to it as a "white lady" that holds sway over them. A recurring theme in the history of cocaine is the massive interest people have shown in the drug from its earliest days to the present.

What Is Cocaine?

Most people are used to thinking of cocaine as a white, powderlike substance—its most common form. That white powder is the extract distilled from the dried leaf of the shrub *Erythroxylon coca*, or the coca plant. Snorting cocaine up the nose is the best known method of ingesting the drug, but cocaine can also be mixed with liquid and injected, or rubbed onto the gums or other mucous membranes, through which it is absorbed.

Cocaine is a stimulant, providing a feeling of euphoria and exhilaration that can last minutes or hours. Cocaine is psychologically addictive: Users tend to crave the cocaine high over and over again. As one cocaine user testifies: "I have a decent job, I attend college at night and I have my own apartment and car. I appear to be doing all right, I even used to think I could just stop using coke when I wanted to, but I can't. I still get sweaty palms and want to jump up and down at the thought of doing some."[1]

Lady Coca

Before cocaine was discovered in the mid-nineteenth century the world knew only coca. The plant is native to South America, and the Incan Indians made "Lady Coca," as they called it, an integral part of their culture. When Europeans arrived in Peru and Bolivia in the fifteenth and sixteenth centuries, they documented the energy-giving properties that come from chewing the dried coca leaf and quickly realized the potential of coca as a cash crop. Today, however, coca has a very different reputation in the United States, where it is viewed mainly as the source from which cocaine is extracted. The federal government has worked closely with the governments of Colombia, Peru, and Bolivia to put a massive coca-eradication program into place.

Many argue that the differences between coca and cocaine are vast. One could equate the effects of coca versus the effects of cocaine to drinking a cup of coffee versus injecting pure caffeine directly into your veins. Much of the literature surrounding coca—personal accounts, historical writings, even medical reports—is positive, as compared to the generally negative view of cocaine. Modern Americans who have tried coca-chewing report gentle stimulating sensations and few, if any, adverse effects. Today's South Americans still integrate coca into their culture. How did this plant, whose reputation was gentle and healthful, make the transition into the dangerous plant that coca is seen as today?

From Coca to Cocaine

In 1860 German chemist Albert Niemann succeeded in distilling cocaine from the coca leaf. Both the medical community and the general public soon came to view the new drug as both harmless and useful. Three years later a pharmacist named Angelo Mariani produced a drink of coca extract (cocaine) dissolved in wine, which he called "Vin Mariani" and which was one of the first cocaine products available to the public. Reports began to appear, testifying to the new drug's energizing effects. In 1885 a druggist in Georgia responded to the temperance movement by creating a nonalcoholic cocaine drink that he called "Coca-Cola." At the same time, the medical community found that cocaine, when applied to the mucous membranes and the surface of the eye, acted as an excellent anesthetic.

There were a few concerns about the possibility of cocaine being either harmful or addictive. For example, in 1886 the *Cincinnati Times-Star* warned:

> When cocaine was discovered, the medical world exclaimed, "Thank Heaven!" But, useful as it is, it is also dangerous, especially when its use is perverted from the deadening of pain for surgical operations, to the stimulation and destruction of the human body. Its first effects are soothing and captivating, but the thralldom is the most horrible slavery known to man. J.L. Stephens, M.D., of Lebanon, Ohio, was interviewed by our reporter yesterday at the Grand Hotel, and during the conversation the doctor said, "The cocaine habit is a thousand times worse than the morphine and opium habits, and you would be astonished," he said, "if you knew how frightfully the habit is increasing."[2]

However, substantial fears about cocaine did not begin to arise until the early years of the twentieth century, when it became clear that the drug was indeed dangerously habit-forming.

Cocaine became regulated in 1914, when it was included in the list of drugs prohibited without a doctor's prescription in the Harrison Narcotic Act. For the first time, coca and its offspring, the "miracle drug" cocaine, began to take on different shades of reputation, beginning the slide toward the modern-day knowledge of the drug.

By the 1970s cocaine was very much a part of popular culture. The relative expense of the drug ensured its place in the hip discos and nightclubs of the time. Cocaine was everywhere. Woody Allen sneezed a cloud of it in the hit movie *Annie Hall*. Frank Zappa, the Rolling Stones, and the Grateful Dead immortalized the drug in their song lyrics. Fancy cocaine paraphernalia abounded: cocaine spoons for snorting, cocaine vials, even cocaine T-shirts. The government mostly ignored the drug—it was illegal, but it was not considered a particular cause for alarm. All of this would soon change with the creation of the substance that solidified cocaine's reputation as one of the most dangerous modern illegal narcotics.

Americans' view of cocaine was transformed forever with

the creation of crack in the 1970s. A new method of using the drug had already been discovered: freebasing, crack's predecessor. Freebasers mixed powder cocaine with ether and smoked the mixture in a pipe. However, ether is highly flammable, a problem that became apparent when popular comedian Richard Pryor set himself on fire trying to freebase. Users discovered that mixing cocaine with baking soda produced small "rocks" that could also be smoked without the risk of fire. Crack cocaine was born, and its use quickly spread.

In the same way that cocaine is a more intense and therefore more addictive form of coca-chewing, crack is a more intense and therefore more addictive form of cocaine. Smoking crack provides a few minutes of an incredibly intense feeling of euphoria, overloading the pleasure centers in the brain. Users find themselves craving the feeling over and over again. Some become addicted after one use. In addition, crack is relatively easy to make from powder cocaine, so by the early 1980s it was widely available.

By the end of the twentieth century, crack use encouraged hundreds of media reports investigating this new form of cocaine. The drug quickly became linked to the African American community, particularly that of the inner cities. New words became a part of the American lexicon: "crackhouse," "crack whore," "crack baby." President George H.W. Bush made crack the center of his National Drug Control Strategy, with his newly launched War on Drugs. America feared a loss of an entire generation to crack. Cocaine had reached its nadir.

America's War on Cocaine

In the twenty-first century, the United States finds itself back where the story of cocaine began: with coca in Bolivia, Colombia, and Peru. After decades of battling cocaine and crack within the country, the federal Office of National Drug Control Strategy and its director John Walters have gone back to the source. Since 2000, the United States has increased its efforts to eradicate South American coca crops that will find their way to the United States in the form of cocaine.

Just as coca once meant life to the Incans, so today coca means money and existence to the peasants who farm it. Those growing illegal coca are reluctant to give it up, as they are paid well by drug lords who buy the plant for processing into cocaine and exportation to the U.S. market. Those who grow the drug legally are targeted indiscriminately. In testimony before the Council on Hemispheric Affairs, a Bolivian activist offers a peasant's view:

> The coca leaf is a part of our culture. The [Bolivian] government should halt coca eradication until it can make a distinction between those who grow it for legal rather than illegal purposes. This should not be a war against farmers trying to survive, but rather against drug dealers. We have created a legal coca leaf market. . . . But we have lost this market because of the government's coca eradication policies. The government has been utilizing its resources to target us as terrorists . . . the coca leaf is as harmless as any other crop.[3]

Drug lords and their armies battle the government soldiers, who alternately battle or cooperate with U.S. troops, with the impoverished coca growers caught in the middle. Yet, the United States remains determined to completely eradicate illegal coca crops throughout Latin America.

The Future of Cocaine

New treatments are constantly being tested to help cocaine addicts, with pharmacology playing an especially prominent role. Vigabatrin, a medication long used to treat epilepsy in the United States, has shown promise in treating cocaine abusers and in 2004 was set to enter the first of many large-scale clinical trials. Studies have also found that a medicine usually used for alcohol addiction, disulfiram, has been effective in combating cocaine addiction as well. Twelve-step and rehab programs aimed at cocaine users abound.

As all of this attention demonstrates, cocaine is still very much alive and present in the United States. In 2006 cocaine will mark the one hundredth anniversary of the first law recognizing its dangers and restricting its use. Lady Coca still grows green on the hills of the Andes, however, and the cocaine extracted from it still enthralls addicts and confounds the governments that work to eradicate it.

Notes

1. Jenn, "Maybe I'm an Addict," Erowid Experience Vaults, June 14, 2000. www.erowid.org/experiences/exp.php?ID=1809.
2. *Cincinnati Times-Star*, "The Cocaine Habit: The Worst Slavery Known—New Revelations of Power," November 20, 1886.
3. Council on Hemispheric Affairs, "On the Record: Leonida Zurita Vargas," *Washington Report on the Hemisphere*, May 12, 2003.

CHAPTER ONE

Coca to Cocaine:
Early Discoveries
and Reactions

Slavery and Adoration: Early Incan Coca Culture

Wade Davis

Wade Davis traveled throughout the Amazon for over a year with his partner Timothy Plowman, studying the coca plant in preparation for writing the book from which this excerpt is taken. Davis holds degrees in anthropology and biology, as well as a PhD in ethnobotany from Harvard University. Here, he offers a history of the Incan people who considered coca a holy and sacred plant, integral to almost every aspect of their culture. When the passage begins, Davis has just completed an all-night bus journey to the remote hill town of Huancavelica in Peru.

Morning in Huancavelica revealed a small colonial town surrounded by barren rocky hills. In addition to the cathedral, beautiful in the soft light, there were seven ornate churches, each betraying a painful history. It was here that the Spaniards found silver and, more important, the mercury they required to smelt the mountain of silver they had found at Potosi in Bolivia. By 1564 Indian slaves from all parts of Peru were being marched into the Huancavelica mines. Beaten with iron bars, torn by whips, they remained underground for a week at a time, strung together in iron collars, working rock faces to extract the daily quota, twenty-five loads per man, one hundred pounds to

Wade Davis, *One River: Explorations and Discoveries in the Amazon Rain Forest.* New York: Simon & Schuster, 1996. Copyright © 1996 by Wade Davis. Reproduced by permission of Simon & Schuster Adult Publishing Group and SLL/Sterling Lord Literistic, Inc.

the load. To their overseers they were not people but "little horses," and when after a few months they stumbled from the pit, chests burning from the toxic dust and vapors, muscles contorted with shakes and tremors, unable to walk, let alone maintain their production, they were simply killed to make room for the next worker. In time mothers began to bury their infant sons alive to save them from the horror of the mines.

In a perverse way the mines played a significant role in the history of coca. The early Spaniards had written glowingly about the plant. In his *Royal Chronicles*, Garcilaso de la Vega wrote that the magical leaf "satisfies the hungry, gives new strength to the weary and exhausted, and makes the unhappy forget their sorrows." Pedro Cieza de León, who traveled throughout the Americas between 1532 and 1550, noted that "when I asked some of these Indians why they carried these leaves in their mouths . . . they replied that it prevents them from feeling hungry, and gives them great vigor and strength. I believe that it has some such effect." The first botanical description of coca, written by the Spanish physician Nicolas Monardes, appeared in a book entitled *Joyfulle News Out of the Newe Founde Worlde, Wherein Is Declared the Virtues of Herbs, Treez, Oyales, Plante and Stones*," translated in 1582 by John Frampton.

The Church Steps In

Predictably, the Catholic Church attempted to outlaw the plant. At ecclesiastical councils held in Lima in 1551 and 1567 the bishops condemned its use as a form of idolatry and secured a royal proclamation declaring the effects of the leaves an illusion of the devil. By then it was too late even for the Church. Too many Spaniards were making fortunes growing and trading coca, and those running the mines had found that without leaves Indians would not work. A face-saving compromise allowed the Church to reverse its position. The cultivation and selling of coca was deemed acceptable, but the use of the leaves in religious ceremonies remained punishable by death. In 1573,

Viceroy Francisco de Toledo removed all controls on secular commerce, and for the next two hundred years, as thousands died in the mines and on the plantations, coca became a mainstay of the colonial economy. Production soared by a factor of fifty, and by the end of the sixteenth century, taxes on coca were providing the Church with much of its revenue.

The dramatic rise in coca production in the years following the Conquest has kept alive one of the most enduring misconceptions about coca; the notion that during the century of Inca domination, the leaves were available only to the ruling elite. Garcilaso de la Vega was perhaps the first to make the claim,

THE HISTORY 🔖 OF DRUGS

The Earliest Mention of Coca

Nicholas Monardes was a Spanish doctor who traveled to Peru and found the Peruvian Indians using a plant he had never seen before: the coca bush. His 1577 botanical description, written in archaic English, is the earliest recorded mention of coca in any text.

I was desirous to see that hearbe so celebrated of the Indians, so many yeres past, whiche they doe call the Coca, whiche they doe sow and till with muche care, and diligence, for because they doe use it for their pleasures, which we will speake of.

The use of it amongst the Indians is a thing generall, for many thinges, for when they doe travaill by the waie, for neede and for their content when they are in their houses, thei use it in this forme. Thei take Cokles or Oisters, in their shelles, and they doe burne them and grinde them, and after they are burned they remaine like Lyme, verie small grounde, and they take of the Leves of the Coca, and they chawe them in their Mouthes, and as they goe chawyng, they goe mingling with it of that pouder made of the shelles in suche sorte, that they make it like to a Paste, taking lesse of the Pouder then of the Hearbe, and of this Paste they make certaine small Bawles rounde, and they put them to drie, and when they will use of them, they take a little and it has since been parroted in nearly every popular account of pre-Columbian Peru. Though the idea has obvious appeal, especially to those critical of the contemporary use of the leaves, evidence for such a monopoly is, in fact, rather sketchy. The Inca did exert control over the production and distribution of various agricultural items including coca, according to many of the early chroniclers who visited the imperial capital. But it is less clear whether their observations of court life in Cuzco [the capital city of Peru] based largely on testimony of Inca nobles, reflect what was going on in the outlying areas of the empire. The history of coca would suggest otherwise.

Ball in their mouthe, and they chawe hym: passing hym from one parte to an other, procuring to conserve him all that they can, and that beyng doen, they doe retourne to take an other, and so they goe, using of it all the tyme that they have neede, whiche is when they travaill by the waie, and especially if it be by waies where is no meate, or lacke of water. For the use of these little Bawles dooe take the hunger and thurste from them, and they say that they dooe receive substaunce, as though that they did eate. At other times thei use of them for their pleasure, although that they labour not by the waie, and thei doe use the same Coca alone, chawing it and bringing it in their mouthes, from one side to another, until there be no vertue remainyng in it, and then they take an other.

When thei will make them selves dronke, and bee out of judgemente, thei mingle with the Coca the leaves of the Tabaco, and thei doe chewe them all together, and thei goe as thei were out of their wittes, like as if thei were dronke whiche is a thyng that dooeth geve them greate contentement to bee in that sorte. Surely it is a thyng of greate consideration, to see how the Indians are so desirous to bee deprived of their wittes, and to bee without understandyng.

Nicholas Monardes, *Joyfull Newes Out of the Newe Founde Worlde*. Trans. John Frampton. London: Constable, 1925, pp. 31–32.

The Role of Coca in Incan Life

It is true, of course, that the Inca revered coca above all other plants. For them it was a living manifestation of the divine; its place of cultivation a natural sanctuary approached by all mortals on bended knee. Unable to grow the leaves at the high elevation of Cuzco, successive rulers ordered plantations to be replicated in gold and silver, in delicate gardens enclosed by temple walls. Coca figured prominently in every aspect of ritual and ceremonial life. Before a journey, priests tossed leaves into the air to propitiate the gods. At the Coricancha, the Court of Gold, the Temple of the Sun, sacrifices were made to the plant, and supplicants only could approach the altar if they had coca in their mouths. The future was read in the venation of leaves and in the flow of green saliva on fingers, by soothsayers and diviners who had acquired their knowledge by surviving a bolt of lightning. At initiation young Inca nobles competed in ardous foot races, while maidens offered coca and *chicha*. At the end of the ordeal each runner was presented with a *chuspa* filled with the finest of leaves as a symbol of his new manhood.

Coca in Marriage and Death

Long caravans carrying as many as three thousand large baskets of leaves regularly moved between lowland plantations and the valleys leading to Cuzco. Without coca, armies could not be maintained or marched across the vast expanse of the empire. Coca allowed the imperial runners, or *chasquis*, to relay messages four thousand miles in a week. When the court orators, or *yaravecs*, were called upon to recite the history of the Inca at ceremonial functions, they were aided only by a system of knotted strings, or *quipus*, and coca to stimulate the memory. In fields priests and farmers offered leaves to bless the harvest. A suitor presented coca to the family of the bride. Official travelers lay spent quids of leaves on rock cairns dedicated to Pachamama and placed at intervals along the paths of the empire. The sick and dying kept leaves at hand, for if coca was the last taste in a person's mouth before death, the path to paradise was assured.

Coca Beyond the Incans

But just as the Inca venerated the plant, so, too, did the other peoples of the Andes. The earliest archaeological evidence suggests that coca was used on the coast of Peru by 2000 B.C. Actual leaves that can be botanically identified as Trujillo [city in Peru] coca have been dated to A.D. 600. Lime pots, lime dippers, and ceramic figurines depicting humans chewing leaves have been found at virtually every major site from every era of pre-Columbian civilization on the coast, Nazca, Paracas, Moche, Chimu. The very word coca is derived not from Quechua [official language of the Incan Empire] but from Aymara, the language spoken by the descendants of Tiwanaku, the empire that predated the Inca on the altiplano [a high plateau] and in the basin of Titicaca by five hundred years. The root word is *khoka*, a simple term meaning bush or tree, thus implying that the source of the sacred leaves is the plant of all plants. Evidence suggests that an active trade in coca was established in the Bolivian highlands as early as A.D. 400, a thousand years before the dramatic expansion of the Inca.

The unique genius of the Inca, and the key to the power of their rule, was their ability to incorporate a remarkably diverse population by assimilating local rulers, absorbing religious ideas, manipulating regional animosities, and establishing new relationships of authority based on ancient notions of exchange—all the time working with local institutions to promote the expansion of their empire. When necessary they could respond ruthlessly, annihilating rebellious tribes, shifting populations to distant lands, and pacifying new conquests by transplanting entire colonies of loyal subjects. Rarely, however, did they violate ancient traditions or institutions that posed no threat to the integrity of the empire. Given this pat-

tern, it seems extremely unlikely that they would have prohibited or been able to suppress a cultural practice as vital and
fundamental as the use of coca. The production and distribution of the plant no doubt came under control, and its sacred
role within areas close to the capital may well have been cir-
cumscribed. On the fields and slopes of the Andes, however,
the plant almost certainly continued to be employed as it always had been: as a mild and essential stimulant in a harsh
and unforgiving landscape.

A European Perspective on Coca in Sixteenth-Century Peru

Garcilaso de la Vega

Garcilaso de la Vega was a Spaniard who lived among the Incan people in Peru during the first part of the sixteenth century. In his life's masterpiece, *Royal Commentaries of the Incas*, excerpted here, Garcilaso discusses the coca plant in detail, describing it as useful and nourishing. By this time, coca was being farmed on massive plantations, run by the Spanish settlers and worked by native laborers. The Europeans found coca as wonderful as the Incans did, but for very different reasons. The income of the bishop of the Catholic Church in the Peruvian capital came almost entirely from the taxes the farmers paid on their coca crops. For the church officials and many others, coca meant wealth.

It would not be right to pass over the herb the Indians call *cuca* and the Spaniards *coca*, which was and still is the chief source of wealth of Peru for those who are engaged in the trade: we should indeed give a full account of it, such is the esteem in which the Indians hold it by reason of the many remarkable virtues they had discovered in it of old, and the many more that the Spaniards have found in applying it to medicine. Padre

Garcilaso de la Vega, *Royal Commentaries of the Incas, and General History of Peru, Part One*, translated by Harold V. Livermore. Austin: University of Texas Press, 1966.

[Father, a priest] Blas Valera, a close observer who spent many years in Peru and left it more than thirty years after I did, writes of both kinds of use, as one who had personal experience of them: I shall simply repeat what his Paternity has to say, and later add the few points he omitted, so as not to run to length by going into detail. He says:

Coca is a certain small tree as big and as high as a vine. It has few branches, but many delicate leaves as broad and half as long as one's thumb. They have a good, but not a soft smell. Indians and Spaniards alike call the leaves *cuca*. It is so agreeable to the Indians that they prefer it above gold, silver, and precious stones. They display great care and diligence in planting it and greater in harvesting it. They pluck the leaves by hand and dry them in the sun; and when so dried they are eaten by the Indians, but they do not swallow them, merely savoring the taste and swallowing the juice. The great usefulness and effect of coca for laborers is shown by the fact that the Indians who eat it are stronger and fitter for their work: they are often so satisfied by it that they can work all day without eating. Coca protects the body from many ailments, and our doctors use it in powdered form to reduce the swelling of wounds, to strengthen broken bones, to expel cold from the body or prevent it from entering, and to cure rotten wounds or sores that are full of maggots. And if it does so much for outward ailments, will not its singular virtue have even greater effect in the entrails of those who eat it? It has another great value, which is that the income of the bishop, canons, and other priests of the cathedral church of Cuzco [the main city] is derived from the tithe on the coca leaf, and many Spaniards have grown rich, and still do, on the traffic in this herb. Nevertheless, some people, ignoring these facts, have spoken and written strongly against this little bush, moved only by the fact that in former times the heathens offered coca to their idols, as some wizards and diviners still do: because of this it is maintained that the use of coca should be completely suppressed and prohibited. This would certainly be good counsel if the Indians merely offered this herb and nothing else to the Devil. But the former heathen (and the idolaters of today) sacrificed crops, vegetables, and fruits that grow below ground and above, and offered their drink and cold water, and wool, and their garments, and cattle, and a great deal else, in short all they might possess, and as they cannot be deprived of all these things, neither can they of coca. They should be instructed to abhor superstition and serve truly one God, availing themselves of all these things in a Christian fashion.

Thus far Father Blas Valera.

Observations of the Plant

To supply what is missing for full measure, we may add that the bushes are as high as a man. They are grown by placing the seed in a nursery as is done with greenstuffs. Small holes are dug for the plants, as for vines, and they are layered like the vine. Great care is taken that no root however small is bent, for this is enough to cause the whole plant to wither. The leaves are plucked, each branch being taken separately between the fingers, which are run along it as far as the new shoot, which must be left or the whole branch shrivels. Both sides of the leaf are exactly like that of the arbutus in color and shape, but they are very thin and it would take three or four of them to equal the arbutus in thickness. I am glad to find objects of Spain that can be so appropriately compared with those of my own country yet which do no exist there: it is thus much easier for those on both sides to understand and know one another. When the leaves have been plucked they are dried in the sun; they are not completely dried or they lose most of their greenness which is much prized, and turn to dust because of their delicacy; nor must they remain very damp, or they grow moldy and rot in the baskets in which they are packed for carriage. They must thus be dried to a point between these extremes. The baskets are made of split canes of which there are plenty, both large and small, in those provinces of the Antis. The outsides of the baskets are covered with the leaves of the thick canes, which are more than a *tercia* [third] broad and more than half a vara [twig] long; thus the coca is prevented from getting wet; for water soon damages it. The baskets are woven with a special kind of hemp that grows in the district. When one considers the quantity of each of these things that is necessary to turn the coca to account, one is rather inclined to give thanks to God for supplying everything wherever it is needed than to attempt to describe it, for it seems incredible. If it were necessary to bring all these requirements from outside, the labor and cost would outweigh the value of the product. The herb is plucked every four months, or thrice yearly, and if the ground is carefully weeded so that all the plants that grow in that hot, wet soil are removed, each harvest is brought forward by a fortnight, so that there are nearly four a year. . . .

The Story of Pantoja

Among the other virtues of coca, it is said to be good for the teeth. With regard to the strength it gives to those who chew it I remember a tale I heard in Peru from a gentleman of quality and merit called Rodrigo Pantoja, who, while travelling from Cuzco to Rímac, came across a poor Spaniard (for there are also poor people over there as there are here) who was walking along with a little daughter of two years old on his back. Pantoja knew him and they fell into conversation.

The gentleman asked: "Why are you burdened like that?"

The other replied: "I have no means to hire an Indian to carry the little girl, so I'm carrying her myself."

At this Pantoja looked at the man's mouth and saw it was full of coca, and as in those days the Spaniards abhorred everything the Indians ate and drank as if they were idolatries, and especially chewing coca (which seemed a vile thing to do), Pantoja asked: "Then if your need is so great why are you chewing coca as the Indians do, when Spaniards hate and detest the stuff?"

The soldier replied: "Sir, I used to abominate it no less than the rest, but necessity forced me to imitate the Indians and chew it, and I can tell you that if I didn't chew it I couldn't carry this burden. It is because of it that I feel strong and vigorous enough to cope with the task."

Pantoja was surprised at hearing this and repeated the story in many different places. Afterwards the Spaniards were inclined to believe the Indians when they said that they ate the herb because they needed it, and not from greed.

Sigmund Freud and His Experiences with Cocaine

E.M. Thornton

Medical historian E.M. Thornton's book *Freud and Cocaine*, excerpted here, is considered the seminal work on the father of psychoanalysis and his long history as a user of the drug. As a member of the medical community in the 1880s, Freud made regular use of the cocaine that was legal and readily available, ordering his supply from the drug manufacturer Merck. Early in his career, Freud became concerned about his good friend, Ernst von Fleischl-Marxow, who had become addicted to morphine. Freud provided cocaine as a restorative for Fleischl, having first tested it on himself with no ill effects. Thornton writes that by 1884 Freud was recommending cocaine for a variety of disorders, while at the same time denying that the drug had addictive properties. Freud amended this view a few years later, when cocaine addiction first became widespread.

In the spring of 1884 an ambitious young Freud was casting around for some brilliant discovery which would bring his name to prominence in the competitive medical world of Vienna. But in Freud's case the most pressing motivation was the furtherance of his marriage plans to Martha Bernays [his fiancée] as soon as he could reasonably expect to be able to support a wife and family. He was then still only an impecunious house officer in the hospital, his appointment to the rank of *Privatdozent* [private lecturer] still in the future. At this crucial time in his life he came across a paper by a German army surgeon, Theodor Aschenbrandt, reporting his experiences with cocaine. . . .

Searching for previous references in the medical literature to cocaine, Freud's attention was drawn to a paper by W.H. Bentley in an obscure journal, *The Therapeutic Gazette* of Detroit, reporting the author's success in weaning opium addicts and alcoholics from their habituation by the use of a preparation of the coca plant produced by the American firm of Parke, Davis and Co. This was of special interest to Freud in view of the condition of his friend and colleague [Ernst] von Fleischl-Marxow who had resorted to morphine for the intolerable pain he suffered and was now experiencing the most extreme consequences of addiction. Freud determined to investigate the substance for himself. "Perhaps others are working at it; perhaps nothing will come of it," he wrote to his fiancée. "But I shall certainly try it, and you know that when one perseveres, sooner or later one succeeds. We do not need more than one such lucky hit to be able to think of setting up house."

The cost of the drug was prohibitive but nevertheless Freud ordered some from the house of Merck. He immediately tested it on himself, taking a twentieth of a gramme, and was pleased to find that it turned his bad mood into cheerfulness and gave him a feeling of having dined well. From its action in obliterating all sense of hunger he deduced that cocaine acted as a gastric anaesthetic, suggesting its use in various gastric conditions and as an anti-emetic. In the hope of weaning Fleischl from his addiction he gave him a quantity. Clutching at the new drug [according to Freud biographer Ernest Jones] "like a drunken man", within a few days Fleischl was taking it regularly, Freud himself, convinced of the harmlessness of this "magical drug", began to take small doses regularly "against depression and against indigestion". He sent some to Martha to make her strong and give her rosy cheeks. He pressed the drug on friends and colleagues both for themselves and their patients, and gave it to his sisters. "In short," wrote Jones, "looked at from the vantage point of our present knowledge, he was rapidly becoming a public menace."

Publishing *Über Coca*

The result of these sporadic and scientifically uncontrolled researches was the paper *Über Coca* which appeared in the July 1884 issue of *Centralblatt für die Gesammte Therapie*. As aptly commented by D.F. Musto, "papers about cocaine assert that everyone should try it, but also impatiently question the motives of those who disagree". Freud's paper is a good example of the genre. He describes his own self-experimentation and the sudden exhilaration experienced a few minutes after taking cocaine, with first a slackening, then an increase in pulse rate. He goes on to describe "the effects of cocaine in others, mostly people my own age" and describes their exhilaration and euphoria which he considered "the normal euphoria of a healthy person", and increased capacity for work. "Long-lasting intensive mental or physical work can be performed without fatigue", he said, "it is as though the need for food and sleep, which otherwise makes itself felt peremptorily at certain times of the day, were completely banished." A meal, though eaten without revulsion, was clearly felt to be superfluous under the effects of cocaine. During the first hours of the coca effect it was not possible to sleep, he continued, but this sleeplessness was in no way distressing.

Ernest Jones comments that the essay was written as if Freud was in love with the content itself. "He used expressions uncommon in a scientific paper", wrote Jones, "such as 'the most gorgeous excitement' that animals display after an injection of cocaine, and administered an 'offering' of it rather than a 'dose'; he heatedly rebuffed the 'slander' that had been published about this precious drug." Jones' translations in this passage have been disputed, but reading the paper one must agree that the presentation is unusual. Freud himself referred to it in a letter to his fiancé as "a song of praise to this magical substance". Viewed objectively as a scientific paper *Über Coca* has many deficiencies. Though the review of the previous literature is comprehensive and appears accurate, the remainder of the paper is vague and disorganised. No information is given on the number of subjects treated, the dosages employed and the duration of the treatment. Beyond a brief mention of the variations in pulse rate, Freud omits reference to other important measurements such as blood pressure readings, temperature recordings and so on. He makes no mention of the dilation of the pupils probably present in those treated. In the section listing the effects of the drug he goes back and forth between his own subjects and those reported in the previous literature in a disorganised fashion. One must agree with Jones' unspoken inference that much of Freud's enthusiasm for cocaine arose from the euphoria engendered by the drug itself.

The Love Affair Continues

Freud's list of indications for the drug were, in this paper, comparatively few. But he was always seeking new applications for it, and before long was recommending it for everything from diabetes to seasickness—a truly universal panacea. Here he merely recommends cocaine as a stimulant especially useful in situations such as mountaineering, war conditions, etc., declaring it to be a "far more potent and far less harmful stimulant than alcohol": he recommends its use to psychiatrists in conditions such as neurasthenia; declares its benefits in various gastric and intestinal disorders and in cases of "cachexia" (state of general ill health and malnutrition). He states that it increased tolerance to mercury (then the only treatment for syphilis) and was therefore of value in this disease. Discussing the use of the drug in the treatment of morphine addiction he refers to cocaine as an "antidote" to morphine, mentioning the case of a man—almost certainly Fleischl—in whom morphine was successfully withdrawn without any of the symptoms experienced when this was attempted before, adding that "after ten days he was able to dispense with the coca treatment altogether". He further recommends the drug as an aphrodisiac, saying that the natives of South America represented their goddess of love with coca in her hand and that three of the people to whom he had given cocaine reported "violent sexual excitement". Finally, he mentions briefly the marked anaesthetising effect of the drug when brought into contact with the skin or mucous membranes—but only in connection with diseases of these organs. The use of cocaine as a local anaesthetic as an adjunct to surgery he missed altogether and the discovery was made by another. . . .

THE HISTORY 🍃 OF DRUGS

The Sign of the Four: Sherlock Holmes Injects Cocaine

Sherlock Holmes's creator, Sir Arthur Conan Doyle, regularly depicted the world's most famous detective indulging in cocaine to soothe his tired body and mind—and irritating his assistant, Dr. Watson—as he does here in this excerpt from The Sign of the Four, *published in 1890.*

Sherlock Holmes took his bottle from the corner of the mantelpiece, and his hypodermic syringe from its neat morocco case. With his long, white, nervous fingers he adjusted the delicate needle, and rolled back his left shirtcuff. For some little time his eyes rested thoughtfully upon the sinewy forearm and wrist, all dotted and scarred with innumerable puncture-marks. Finally, he thrust the sharp point home, pressed down the tiny piston, and sank back into the velvet-lined arm-chair with a long sigh of satisfaction.

Three times a day for many months I had witnessed this performance, but custom had not reconciled my mind to it. On the contrary, from day to day I had become more irritable at the

Fleischl Deteriorates

By early 1885, the condition of his friend Fleischl was giving cause for concern. Fleischl had, it was true, been successfully weaned from morphia, but was now in the grip of a far more formidable allegiance to cocaine. By April 1885 he was consuming enormous doses of the drug; Freud noted that he had spent 1,800 marks on it in the past three months, a figure indicating a dosage of a full gramme a day, a hundred times that which Freud was accustomed to take, and then only occasionally. Fleischl had evidently also resumed his use of morphine and was taking both drugs concurrently, a usage that was to emerge as a very characteristic pattern whenever cocaine was used to wean morphine addicts from their former allegiance.

sight, and my conscience swelled nightly within me at the thought that I had lacked the courage to protest. Again and again I had registered a vow that I should deliver my soul upon the subject; but there was that in the cool, nonchalant air of my companion which made him the last man with whom one would care to take anything approaching to a liberty. His great powers, his masterly manner, and the experience which I had had of his many extraordinary qualities, all made me diffident and backward in crossing him.

Yet upon that afternoon, whether it was the Beaune [a type of red wine] which I had taken with my lunch, or the additional exasperation produced by the extreme deliberation of his manner, I suddenly felt that I could hold out no longer.

'Which is it to-day,' I asked, 'morphine or cocaine?'

He raised his eyes languidly from the old black-letter volume which he had opened.

'It is cocaine,' he said, 'a seven-per-cent solution. Would you care to try it?'

Arthur Conan Doyle, *The Sign of the Four*. Oxford, UK: Oxford University Press, 1993, p. 3.

By April, Freud had had to sit up all one night with his friend Fleischl lying in a warm bath by his side—"Every note of the profoundest despair was sounded," he wrote to Martha. On June 8 Freud was telling Martha that the frightful doses had harmed Fleischl greatly, and although he continued to send her cocaine, he warned her against acquiring the habit.

Yet knowing that Fleischl was taking these large doses of cocaine when he was supposed to have ceased its use, Freud read a paper on March 3 at the Physiological Club, and two days later at the Psychiatric Society in which he described what must certainly have been Fleischl's case, as one of "rapid withdrawal from morphine under cocaine"; the habit, he said, had been overcome in twenty days by the use of the latter drug. "No cocaine habituation set in," he claimed, "on the contrary, an increasing antipathy to the use of cocaine was unmistakably evident." He had no hesitation, he continued, in recommending the administration of cocaine for such withdrawal cures in *subcutaneous injections*. This paper was published in the *Medico-Chirurgis Centralblatt* on August 7, 1885. Between its original delivery and its publication, Fleischl's condition had deteriorated still further. By June he had begun to exhibit the classic symptoms of severe cocaine intoxication— attacks of fainting and convulsions, insomnia and behavioural eccentricities, culminating in the characteristic hallucinations of small animals, in this case white snakes crawling over his skin. On June 4, Freud had found him in such a condition— . . . that he went to fetch his physician Breuer, and then stayed the night there, "the most frightful night he had ever spent," he wrote to Martha In this sorry, broken-down state, the once gifted, brilliant, handsome and aristocratic Fleischl lingered for another six painful years before being released by death from his wretched existence. Yet, having been witness to these terrible scenes knowing that Fleischl was still taking morphine as well as cocaine and having warned his fiancée of acquiring the habit, Freud allowed the 1885 paper to go forward for publication in August. Not only that, but Jones, failing to notice

Freud's mendacious reports that Freud was "gratified" when the *Lancet* subsequently abstracted it.

Freud Concedes That Cocaine Is Addictive

Freud was to regret this paper two years later when reports of addiction and its frightful consequences had begun to flow in from all parts of the globe and he was having to defend himself against the accusations of the psychiatrist Erlenmeyer that he had unleashed on the world the third scourge of humanity, the first two being alcohol and morphine. His defence, set out in a paper published in the *Wiener Medizinische Wochenschrift* of July 1895, was somewhat tendentious, laying the chief blame on others. The new use of cocaine was first brought to the general attention of physicians and also, unfortunately, of morphine addiction through the pamphlets of E. Merck Co., Darmstadt, and an extravagant article by Walle in the *Deutsche Medizinalzeitum*. Freud now conceded the fact of addiction to cocaine—a far more dangerous one than that to morphine, he admitted. He cites rapid physical and moral deterioration, hallucinatory states, agitation similar to delirium tremens, and the "chronic persecution mania", as well as the characteristic hallucinations of small animals moving on the skin, effects which must have been only too familiar to him from the case of his friend. He compared its use in the treatment of morphine addiction to "the sad results of trying to cast out the devil by Beelzebub". Many morphine addicts who had until that time held their own life now succumbed to cocaine, he admitted. But these terrible results were only found in morphine addicts, "persons who, already in the grip of one demon are so weak in will power, so susceptible, that they would misuse, and indeed have misused, any stimulant held out to them". Cocaine, he asserted, "has claimed no other, no victim on its own". It was a rash statement to make without supporting evidence. Reports from all over the world were soon to prove him tragically wrong.

Freud's second line of defense was that the harmful effects of the drug were due to its having been *injected subcutaneously* instead of taken by mouth, as he had recommended. Unfortunately, *he had*, in the 1885 paper, recommended these injections. This paper, as Jones relates, was subsequently suppressed by Freud. It appeared neither in his list of publications submitted with his application for the title of Professor in 1897, nor was it found among his collection of reprints after his death. Yet there were those whose memories must have gone back to this paper—[Ernst] Brücke, for instance, Freud's former chief and Fleischl's present one, who would, as a physiologist, almost certainly have attended the meeting of the Physiology Club at which it was first read and who was witness to the terrible scenes with Fleischl when he was supposed to have been cured. Was it for this reason that Freud wrote later in the *Interpretation of Dreams* of the "terrible gaze of his eyes", eyes of steely blue that were to haunt him for years to come?

Interestingly, the 1887 paper gives us some information on Freud's own experience with cocaine. He claims to have taken the drug himself "for some months" without ill effect or any desire for its continued use. "On the contrary, there occurred more frequently than I should have liked, an aversion to the drug, which was sufficient cause of curtailing its use." This would indicate that by 1887 Freud had ceased to use the drug himself.

The Joy of Cocaine

William A. Hammond

During the late nineteenth century, many Americans viewed cocaine as an exciting new drug. Dr. William A. Hammond, a leading neurologist and former U.S. surgeon general, was among those eager to try it. Hammond was well respected in his field and was frequently consulted by the press on issues such as insanity, castration, and the mental state of the murderer Jack the Ripper. In 1887 Hammond offered the following speech to the Medical Society of Virginia. In it, he describes his experiments on himself with different dosages of cocaine. He describes feeling exhilaration after injecting himself with increasingly large amounts of cocaine, and he recommends the drug as a treatment for depression. Though he admits to taking a near-fatal dose at one point, Hammond nonetheless vigorously argues against the existence of the so-called cocaine habit, as speculated on by his fellow doctors at the time.

It is not my intention to consume the time of the Society by entering into the clinical history of the erythroxylon coca, or of the voluminous literature of which it and its active principle have been the subject; neither shall I devote much attention to the observations, interesting though they be, of other physicians and surgeons. I shall confine my remarks, therefore, almost entirely to an account of my own experience with these very important remedies. That experience, based as it is upon the results obtained by the administrations of coca and its preparations to others, as well as those drawn from a large personal experience of coca and the hydrochlorate of cocaine,

William A. Hammond, "Coca: Its Preparations and Their Therapeutical Qualities, with Some Remarks on the So-Called Cocaine Habit," *Virginia Medical Monthly*, November 1887.

will I trust be of interest to the members of the Medical Society of Virginia. . . .

Effects of the Self-Experiment

About two years ago I undertook a series of experiments with this agent on myself, with the object of obtaining more satisfactory information relative to its action than it seemed possible for me to get otherwise. I began by injecting a grain of the substance under the skin of the forearm, the operation being performed at 8 o'clock, P.M.

The first effect ensued in about five minutes, and consisted of a pleasant thrill which seemed to pass through the whole body. This lasted about ten minutes and shortly after its appearance was accompanied by a sensation of fullness in the head and heat of the face. There was also noticed a decided acceleration of the pulse with increase of force. This latter symptom was probably, judging from subsequent experiments, the very first to ensue, but my attention being otherwise engaged it was overlooked. On feeling the pulse five minutes after making the injection, it was found to be 91, while immediately before the operation it was only 82.

With these physical phenomena there was a sense of exhilaration and an increase of mental activity that were well marked and not unlike in character those that ordinarily follow a glass or two of champagne. I was writing at the time, and I found that my thoughts flowed with increased freedom, and were unusually well expressed. The influence was well felt for two hours, when it gradually began to fade. At 12 o'clock, four hours after the injection, I went to bed, feeling, however, no disposition to sleep. I lay awake till daylight, my mind actively going over all the events of the previous day. When I at last fell asleep it was only for two or three hours, and then I awoke with a severe frontal headache. This passed off after breakfast.

On the second night following, at 7 o'clock, I injected two grains of the hydrochlorate of cocaine into the skin of the fore-

arm. At that time the pulse was 84, full and soft. In four minutes and a half it had increased to 92, was decidedly stronger
than before and somewhat irregular in rhythm. The peculiar
thrill previously mentioned was again experienced. All the
phenomena attendant on the first experiment were present in
this, and to an increased degree. In addition there were twitch-
ing of the muscles of the face, and a slight tremor of the hands
noticed especially in writing. In regard to the mental manifes-
tations there was a similar exhilaration as in the last experiment, but much more intense in character. I felt a great desire
to write, and did so with a freedom and apparent clearness
that astonished me. I was quite sure, however, at the time, that
on the following morning, when I came to read it over, I would
find my lucubrations to be of no value; I was therefore agree-
ably disappointed when I came to pursue it, after the effects of
the drug had passed off, that it was entirely coherent, logical,
and as good, if not better in general character, as anything I
had previously written.

The effects of this dose did not disappear till the middle of
the next day, nor until I had drunk two or three cups of strong
coffee. I slept little or none at all, the night being passed in
tossing from side to side of the bed, and in thinking of the most
preposterous subjects. I was, however, at no time unconscious,
but it seemed as though my mind was to some extent perverted
from its usual course of action. The heat of the head was great-
est at about 12 o'clock, and at that time my pulse was 112, the
highest point reached. I had no headache until after arising,
and the pain disappeared in the course of the morning.

Four nights subsequently I injected four grains of the hydrochlorate of cocaine into the skin of the left forearm. The effects were similar in almost every respect with those of the
other experiments except that they were much more intense.
The mental activity was exceedingly great, and in writing, my
thoughts as before appeared to be lucidly and logically expressed. I wrote page after page, throwing the sheets on the
floor without stopping to gather them together. When, how-

ever, I came to look them over on the following morning, I found that I had written a series of high flown sentences altogether different from my usual style, and bearing upon matters in which I was not in the least interested. The result was very striking as showing the difference between a large and excessive dose of the drug, and yet it appeared to me at the time that what I was writing consisted of ideas of very superior character and expressed with a beauty of diction of which I was in my normal condition altogether incapable.

The disturbance of the action of the heart was also exceedingly well marked, and may be described best by the word "tumultuous." At times, beginning within three minutes after the injection, and continuing with more or less intensity all through the night, the heart beat so rapidly that its pulsations could not be counted, and then its action would suddenly fall to a rate not exceeding 60 in a minute, every now and then dropping a beat. This irregularity was accompanied by a disturbance of respiration of a similar character, and by a sense of oppression in the chest that added greatly to my discomfort.

Pushing Overdose Limits

Up to this time I certainly had not taken a poisonous dose of cocaine, or one that had produced any serious inconvenience. My experience had satisfied me that a much larger dose than any I had up to that time injected might, in my case at least, be taken with impunity. A consideration of the phenomena observed appeared to show that the effects produced by 12 grains were not very much more pronounced than those following 6 grains. I determined, therefore, to make one more experiment, and to inject 18 grains. I knew that in a case of attempted suicide 23 grains had been taken into the stomach without seemingly injurious effect, and that in another case 32 grains were taken within the space of three hours without symptoms following of greater intensity than those I had experienced.

I had taken the doses of 8, 10 and 12 grains in divided quantities, and this dose of 18 grains I took in four portions within five minutes of each other. At once an effect was produced upon the heart, and before I had taken the last injection the pulsations were 140 to the minute and characteristically irregular. In all the former experiments, although there was great mental exaltation, amounting at times almost to delirium, it was nevertheless distinctly under my control, and I am sure that at any time under the influence of a sufficiently powerful incentive I could have obtained entire mastery over myself, and have acted after my normal manner. But in this instance, within five minutes after taking the last injection, I felt that my mind was passing beyond my control, and that I was becoming an irresponsible agent. I did not feel exactly in a reckless mood, but I was in such a frame of mind as to be utterly regardless of any calamity or danger that might be impending over me. I do not think I was in a particularly combative condition, but I was elated and possessed of a feeling as though exempt from the operation of deleterious influences. I do not know how long this state of mind continued, for I lost consciousness of all my acts within, I think, half an hour after finishing the administration of the dose. Probably, however, other moods supervened, for the next day when I came downstairs, three hours after my usual time, I found the floor of my library strewn with encyclopaedias, dictionaries, and other books of reference, and one or two chairs overturned. I certainly was possessed of the power of mental and physical action in accordance with the ideas by which I was governed, for I had turned out the gas in the room and gone upstairs to my bed-chamber and lighted the gas, and put the match used in a safe place, and undressed, laying my clothes in their usual place, had cleaned my teeth and gone to bed. Doubtless these acts were all automatic, for I had done them all in pretty much the same way for a number of years. During the night the condition which existed was, judging from the previous experiments, certainly not sleep, and yet I remained entirely unconscious until 9 o'clock the following morning, when I found myself in bed, with a splitting headache and a good deal of cardiac and respiratory disturbance. For several days afterward I felt the effects of this extreme dose in a certain degree of languor and indisposition to mental or physical exertion; there was also a difficulty in concentrating the attention, but I slept soundly every night without any notable disturbance from dreams.

Evaluating the Self-Experiment

Certainly in this instance I came very near taking a fatal dose, and I would not advise anybody to repeat the experiment. I suppose that if I had taken the whole quantity in one single injection instead of in four, over a period of twenty minutes, the result might have been disastrous. Eighteen grains of cocaine are equivalent to about 3600 grains of coca leaves, and of course, owing to its concentration, capable of acting with very much greater intensity.

I am not aware that a fatal dose of cocaine has yet been indicated by actual fact. Probably 18 grains would kill some people, and perhaps even smaller quantities might, with certain individuals, be fatal. But these are inferences and not facts; but so far as I know there is not an instance on record of a person dying from the administration of cocaine. So far as my experiments extend (and I think it will be admitted that they have gone as far as is safe) I am inclined to think that a dose sufficient to produce death would do so by its action on the heart. Certainly it was there that in my case the most dangerous symptoms were perceived. The rapidity, force, and marked irregularity of the pulse all showed that the innervation of the heart was seriously affected.

It is surprising that no marked influence appeared to be exercised upon the spinal cord or upon the ganglia at the base of the brain. Thus there were no disturbances of sensibility (no anesthesia, no hyperæsthesia) and no interference with motility, except that some of the muscles, especially those of the face, were subjected to slight twitchings. In regard to sight and hearing, I noticed that both were affected, but that while the sharpness of vision was decidedly lessened, the hearing was increased in acuteness. At no time were there any hallucinations.

Injecting Cocaine

Acting from the data thus obtained, I have used the hydrochlorate of cocaine to a considerable extent in my practice, but always by hypodermic injections when employing it in its pure state. For internal administration, I have [dissolved cocaine into] wine in preference; but recognizing the power of the substance when locally applied to mucous membranes to diminish the calibre of the blood-vessels of the part and to produce anesthesia I should use it in certain affections of the stomach upon the same principle as it is at present applied to the nasal mucous membrane, the larynx, and the larynx, should cases requiring its employment come under my observation.

I have derived great benefit from its administration hypodermically in cases of *melancholia*, and in others of *hysteria* characterized by great depression of spirits. In such case a half grain may be injected under the skin, and if necessary the quantity gradually increased to two grains. I have never given more than this quantity to a patient at one time, but I have frequently reached this point without having yet witnessed any deleterious effects. One injection given daily for three or four days will often make the most dismal melancholic cheerful, and what is remarkable is the fact that the improvement is permanent. In the case of a woman strongly hysterical, and who had not spoken a word for several months, a single injection of a grain (a rather large dose to begin with, but one which I thought proper under the circumstances) broke the spell in less than five minutes, and there has up to this date— and nearly a year has elapsed—been no return of any hysterical symptom. . . .

Denying the "Cocaine Habit"

We have heard a good deal of the *cocaine habit*, a habit which I am very sure has *no existence* as such. I do not deny that there are morphi-eaters who, having heard that cocaine is an antidote to the morphia habit, have endeavored to cure themselves with it, and being deprived of full powers of judgment and of will, have ingrafted the cocaine on the morphia habit, producing thereby an exceedingly bad combination. But that there is any such thing as a cocaine habit pure and simple which the individual cannot of his own effort altogether arrest, I emphatically deny. The injection of half a grain to a grain produces a certain degree of mental exhilaration which is pleasurable, and which attends upon a repetition of the dose; but there is no weakening of the will power, such as is produced by morphia, and no craving for the drug such as opium and its preparations cause. I have given it to many patients, male and female, for several weeks continuously, and have never had a single one object to its administration being stopped. There is not so much trouble in ceasing its use as there is in giving up tea or coffee, and nothing like so much as is experienced by those who cease using alcohol or tobacco. Within a space of a few months, Dr. Bosworth, of New York, took, I think, between 500 and 600 grains, and stopped without suffering the least inconvenience.

The Nightmare of Cocaine

Anonymous, identified as "a former 'Snow-Bird'"

By the end of the nineteenth century, cocaine's dangers were well known and the U.S. government had passed the Harrison Narcotics Act, the first law regulating the distribution and possession of narcotic drugs, including cocaine. The following is an account of cocaine addiction published in 1929 by an anonymous writer who refers to himself only as "a former 'snow-bird'" (*snow* was popular slang for cocaine). Throughout the piece, the author curses the drug and laments that he ever tried it. He describes becoming addicted to cocaine while on active duty during World War I. After the war, he was unable to shake the addiction, despite his great desire to be rid of the drug, until finally he isolated himself on a long sea voyage.

In 1917, along with many other Americans, I went to France as an officer in the A.E.F. [American Expeditionary Forces]. I was glad to go; not that I was anxious to fight and die, not that I was possessed of any burning patriotism, but because I saw in the war an opportunity to get away from an unpleasant domestic situation, a situation to which I had failed to adjust myself. In France and at the front I soon learned that cognac was a powerful support for a timid spirit. I was honestly frightened many times. There came an harassing week; rain, mud, shells, no relief; literally Hell. Cognac gone? Spirits lagging! Not exactly frightened but fearful. Oh, for one big drink? But none was there.

A fellow officer of the French army stood beside me in the

Anonymous, "The Nightmare of Cocaine by a Former 'Snow-Bird,'" *North American Review*, vol. 227, April 1929, pp. 418–22.

rain. His spirits were high, he was happy. I saw him occasionally put a pinch of something in his nostrils, and a moment later his eyes were bright, he was levity in the face of disaster, he was confident. I shuddered—snow! We watched our posts hour after hour, the drizzle became sleet, the gray day became foggy dusk, the Germans increased the intensity of their fire, there was a tenseness in the darkness, a raid was imminent. Cognac! I fairly prayed for it, I reached out my hand and my companion smiled as he placed in it the tiny box. I was awkward, but I took one, two quick sniffs of the snowy powder. There was a momentary burning sensation, quick free breaths, a suffusing warmness, and with it my timidity disappeared. The whining shells became louder—I smiled. A few broke near—I laughed. Half an hour later we were successful in driving off a well-organized raid. I patted the shoulder of my French benefactor—God, how I cursed him later! He merely shrugged his shoulders, held out the box, and I accepted it once more.

Excuses! I hear the word. Not at all; I offer none. I wanted relief. I knew exactly what I was doing. I merely substituted cocaine for alcohol, a bad bargain at the best, but at the particular moment the only one possible. No, I write no excuses. I have merely described an incident as it occurred. Unfortunately, cocaine was easy to obtain in France. A small package, conveniently carried in a side pocket, was a long supply and more powerful than bulky bottles of cognac. Alcohol was deserted, cocaine took the whip, and a more pitiless taskmaster man never had. A rotten trade!

Sinking into Addiction

A week later we were relieved and I fell back on my ever present outlet, my voluminous diary. Hour after hour in the rest camp I wrote, wrote of every conceivable subject, of myself, of life, of war, of the soldiers. My pen would lag, ideas would grow leadenfooted; cognac, again plentiful, I scorned; snow—

ever it was snow. The sombre skies of Northern France mattered not; the cold, sodden turf, the driving sleet, the heavy twilight; either they did not exist or were entirely overshadowed by the roseate warmth of my own being—the glow of snow. Mine was another world. Alluring fancies, elusive ideas, a rapid procession; I would try to catch and hold one for my own, but with an aggravating and charming fleetness a new one would crowd the other from view. A thousand pictures flashing across the silver screen of my mind, the endless cinema of stimulated fancy, the pitiless drive of a tireless driver. Yes—yes—I must write that story; many of the aviators had told it, that strange apparition they had seen, her hair flying, her black eyes flashing, spreading a wild courage as she would lead them higher, higher to victory. No, not victory, disaster! Ridiculous, stupid! Here on our side we prayed with vehemence to the God of justice for strength to give those dirty Huns a good drubbing, while over there they did the same thing in exactly the same way. How God must have held His sides and laughed! Far into the night I wrote and dreamed, often until gray dawn came sludgily from the East and the stirrings of life around the barracks announced another day.

The war ended. I was sent to Berlin, where I worked as I never knew one could. There was time for nothing but the daily routine, a thousand petty details, but each one important. Here I made my first and unsuccessful stand against "snow". One month, two months I held out, and my weight was coming back to normal, my appetite returned, I enjoyed long nights of undisturbed sleep. Yes, I missed my fancies, my dreams. I had been haunted from time to time by weird fears; cocaineurs became morally degenerate, physically careless. Would I? Time and again I wondered. But with abstinence came new respect for self; I found time to write a great deal and I note in those old diaries new and sane ideas, a clear outlook which was refreshing after many pages of maudlin and incoherent imaginings. I played polo, I swam, I read. One day I threw an ounce of "snow" into a great pond where a dozen graceful swans were preening themselves. With an inward glow of self satisfaction I walked slowly back to the Hotel Adlon through the gathering dusk.

Two days later the Adjutant handed me orders to return to America for discharge. It was a blow! True, peace had been signed for nearly a year, though I could scarcely realize the fact. I had landed in France in August, 1917; here it was May, 1920, after nearly three years eventful, crowded, and happy after a fashion. I had hoped to go to Poland. In fact I would have gone anywhere on earth to have kept away from New York, the old pictures, the old surroundings again. My blood grew cold. For half a day I wandered the streets. Little groups of German schoolboys with whom I often chatted were unnoticed. New York—I tramped on slowly. America—it meant all that old unhappiness again. There, directly in front of me (how insidiously clever one's unguided feet can be) was the little pharmacy. Two grams? Yes, yes, that would he enough. In an hour I did not care!

Before leaving Berlin I purchased nearly four ounces of cocaine, a small fortune in America. Being an officer I know my own belongings were safe. I had decided.

In Cocaine's Grip

I landed in New York in mid-June. It was late before we were allowed to go ashore; even then I knew I could not go home. Instead I went to a hotel. I must have looked terrible. For nights I had paced the decks of the transport, my "snow" and I. A million illusions had danced from crest to crest of the endless waves. With a killing forcefulness the drug drove my fagged [tired] brain pitilessly, tirelessly. Far out in the utter solitude of spaceless void, out where only souls exist, somewhere there must be peace. I know that at times I was only a dull machine attached to a wandering spirit by the very flimsiest of threads. I would watch the swirling wake at nights, I was tempted to plunge into the restless water. Food was revolting. Sleep impossible. I wrote endlessly. Today I can laugh at those pages. An incoherency understandable only to me, a mendacity which is charmingly naive, and through it all a powdery trail anyone with an experienced eye can detect, the trail of snow!

The clerk assigned me a room, and with genuine concern asked if I were sick and did I wish the house doctor. I mumbled some reply and hastened to the upper floors. For an hour I watched the lights of the city. Home—but not mine. I listened with ears acutely drug-tempered to the many ever present but unannoying sounds of a city. Home? I reached for a vial. One sniff, two, three—funny thing, home. Silly sentimental old codgers wrote about it—folks seemed to like it—if they could write, why not I? For an hour I did. To this day that hour's writing is one of the seven wonders to me. Not a single capital letter, not one punctuation mark, often whole lines without a break for words. It was as if someone had taken a long strip of light-fogged motion picture with unbelievable rapidity and then had translated it into words. Yet from somewhere in my drug-befuddled brain one definite idea took shape, Home? Why not?

I heard the distant ringing, a few hasty words, that was home! Half an hour later my wife, white eyed, horrified, tight-lipped, walked from my room. Her burning, hissing words I still hear. "You degenerate! My God, you are loathsome!" She was right!

Struggling to Break the Hold

Two days later I was normal, but far from well. My fortune, if any, was my education. I needed no strong box. I took my slender savings and there began a search which eventually ended in a little boat yard up the river. I still own that boat; she is my sacred holy of holies, for she carried me out of the world of slavery to a very real freedom. I left my books behind and I would not go back for them. Early one morning I drifted down the Hudson, out past the Goddess who holds high her symbolic torch proclaiming her everlasting message to all the world, and there, one by one, I emptied my boxes of "snow" into the surging waters and silently watched the last fleck of white disappear. With a sigh of real relief I laid my course for sea, caught the first of a light morning breeze, and soon lost the lines of the city in the mistiness. Perhaps a needless gesture, probably cheap dramatics, but it was done honestly and earnestly. Free from any taint we, my boat and I, went to sea and there we stayed.

To write of struggles would be boastful. I recall too vividly the wild exhortations of the "reformed" drunkard as he told in lurid words of the dreadful depth to which he had been dragged by the demon rum. I think there was an element of the braggart in his almost maniacal emotionalism, and certainly a state of mind not far removed from his detested intoxication; he had only made a trade.

It is hard to write of those days for fear the sense of boastfulness will creep in and ruin the truth. There were days when I would lie hour after hour on the deck of the boat, hungrily looking past the top of the swaying mast into that great realm of fancy where lived my many friends. Around me stern reality; that other land was there, but, alas! the door was locked, and the key—my last fleck of "snow" was where I had put it.

Mercifully, Nature usually took a hand, bringing a sudden gale and high seas which demanded long hours of cautious tiller work, much toil on ropes and sails, with at last a warm morning, the storm over; and exhausted I would sleep the clock around. With wholesome fatigue and rest came new strength, so that for weeks I was conscious only of the joy of living and the joy of freedom. I threaded a thousand narrow straits, I explored untold deserted harbors, I saw Voodoo rituals. I tramped the country of Morgan, I sailed the seas of Drake, I sang lustily every song I had ever heard. I was living, I was free. Sometimes with the relentlessness of Javert from nowhere would come a bad day, but I noticed they happened less often. Came a time at last when a year slipped by without one. I had learned. Then and then only I trusted myself in a city. The rest was easy. For nine years "snow" and I have lived apart. At no time have I ever felt a physical call for cocaine, none of the racking struggles of withdrawal.

A Refuge for the Addict

I want no smpathy, I did the one thing which was as logical as were the steps leading to the first contact. But I hear the question, "Is there any way out for the majority of addicts who can't buy a boat and sail the Seven Seas?" Most emphatically, yes!

In approaching the addict himself there should be a sympathetic attitude. Once we understand how and why he began, we are in a position to help him intelligently. Often he is not conscious of any real reason, but I feel certain that it does exist and can be found, and once exposed to clear light the fearfulness often disappears. The next great step is isolation; the addict must be moved to new and wholesome surroundings; old friends, old scenes, old contacts, must be left behind and in the new place there should be hard work a-plenty. Quite naturally it means absolute abstinence from the drug.

I have long dreamed of such a colony, well removed from the world at large, where men can go and find help along the tedious road of rehabilitation. Not a penal colony but a great workshop with work for all, in time self-sustaining, a refuge for those who will come and find the great joy of that greater freedom. Many would never leave but would remain to help others along the way. I know of no finer work that some man of millions could do than to endow such a place. No man could ask for a greater monument!

But I forget. I must finish my story. For four years we stayed at sea, down the Atlantic, across the lovely Carib, meeting a few storms but mostly just good wholesome ocean and plenty of hard work. At last I came home, to my home, mine only. Here I work and the years are full.

An American Invention: Cocaine and Coca-Cola

Paul Gootenberg

Paul Gootenberg is a professor of history and director of Latin American and Caribbean studies at Stony Brook University in New York. He has written extensively about cocaine and its relation to Latin American history, as well as about nineteenth-century Peruvian history. In the following article, Gootenberg discusses the controversy the Coca-Cola corporation engendered in the early twentieth century by including coca in its new "magic drink." Quickly, the company became embroiled with the federal government and antidrug crusaders, while at the same time supplying its increasingly clamorous customers with the cocaine-infused beverage. Most hotly contested was the mysterious "Merchandise No. 5," the formula said to contain coca. The ingredients were supplied by Maywood Chemical, a U.S. company that imported large amounts of coca and later teamed up with Coca-Cola to monitor coca imports in a deal with the federal government. In this article, Gootenberg offers a deep look at these key players and examines communications between drug agencies, the governments of the United States and Peru, and the Coca-Cola corporation itself.

Coca-Cola, the 'big drink', was both a powerful symbol and factor in the rise and fall of American coca. Between 1900 and

Paul Gootenberg, "Secret Ingredients: The Politics of Coca in US-Peruvian Relations, 1915–1965," *The Journal of Latin American Studies*, vol. 36, 2004. Copyright © 2004 by Cambridge University Press. Reproduced by permission.

1920, the Coca-Cola Company transformed from a major target of drug reformers into a crucial government ally. As now documented, the original Coca-Cola formula, concocted by Atlanta pharmacist John S. Pemberton in 1886, was born directly out of the rising American coca culture of the late-nineteenth century, company denials notwithstanding. Coca-Cola began life as 'Peruvian Wine Cola', an open southern imitation of Vin Mariani, the legendary Bordeaux coca tonic that enjoyed fantastic success in Europe from the 1860s. Swiftly spreading into US markets—Mariani's brother opened a New York branch in the 1880s—it won enthusiasts from all walks of life, but most of all among educated 'brain-workers'. . . . Pemberton's Coca-Cola took the wine out, as Atlanta went dry, aiming for a soda-fountain health-craze 'soft' drink. He added caffeine from African kola-nut and ample sugar, making it a kind of over-the-counter 'speed-ball' of the era, though the cocaine content *per se* was modest. (True cocaine lovers still had the market's potent asthma or catarrh 'cures', taken nasally.)

Criticism Begins

Critics—including leading social reformers of the Progressive movement—immediately equated Coca-Cola consumption with 'dope' (and 'Coke' jingles with cocaine abuse). Critics played up on escalating Jim Crow racial fears, with tales of hopped-up southern 'negroes' on soda-fountain binges. Coca-Cola was hardly the problem, but to pre-empt negative publicity, Coca-Cola's legendary president, Asa G. Candler, quietly withdrew cocaine from the product in 1903. Coca-Cola first joined with Schaeffer Alkaloidal Works of Maywood, a small but expert New Jersey concern, since it made political sense for Coca-Cola discreetly to farm out this controversial operation to an independent firm. Schaeffer himself had remarkable roots: a German chemist sent by Boehringer (Mannheim) in 1885–86 to promote cocaine-making in Lima, where Schaeffer likely learned the art of coca extracts, he migrated with his own patents to New Jersey, setting up shop by 1895. Schaeffer specialised in the top-secret 'de-cocainised' leaf extract, soon dubbed Merchandise No. 5, as the fifth of '7X' (or seven mystery) ingredients in coke syrup, sold and sent by the barrel to bottlers throughout the land.

This reform was not enough. In 1906, the FDA's chief chemist, Harvey W. Wiley, began pursuit of Coca-Cola, after muckraking attacks on coca-laced patent medicines. Ironically, the climactic Federal show-trial of Coca-Cola, in Chattanooga Tennessee in 1911–12, centred on charges of fraud: that Coke wilfully duped consumers by still boasting the C-word in its name, which it no longer contained. Coca-Cola won the case, despite expert testimony against it by luminaries such as H.H. Rusby, a towering figure in the botanical history of coca-leaf and editor-in-chief of the US Pharmacopoeia. Vital testimony hinged on the inner nature of Merchandise No. 5 and its secretive 'De-COCAINIZED' coca extract, which Rusby, in extreme doses, had used to kill rabbits. Even after Wiley's defeat, Coca-Cola attracted heat from zealous anti-drug forces (like the WCTU [Women's Christian Temperance Union]) and well into the 1930s marginal critics attributed Coca-Cola's popularity to a concealed dose of addicting cocaine. Company executives debated jettisoning the trace coca flavouring altogether, but allegedly kept it due to their growing 'cult of the formula'.

The Fame of Merchandise No. 5

By 1930 every annual report of the major US drug agency, the reformed Federal Bureau of Narcotics [also called the FBN, the forerunner to the modern Drug Enforcement Agency], contained a conspicuous section devoted to Merchandise No. 5. In part this was for foreign consumption: the Commissioner's annual 'Traffic in Opium and Other Dangerous Drug' statement functioned as a national report to the League of Nations and later UN Narcotics agencies. Coca represented a glaring political dilemma, given the United States' post-1914 zeal in international drug crusades. Domestic politics and informal agreements oiled this bureaucrat pact, in meetings between Col. Levi Nutt [FBN director], Stuart Fuller (the State Department's anti-drug man) and Coca-Cola and Maywood executives. The United States, according to the 1930 report, allows no imports of cocaine, ecgonine (a usable derivative) or their salts, and it prohibits domestic cultivation of coca. But it did allow a unique legal provision for imports of '*non*-medicinal' coca. The Commissioner wielded extraordinary import permits, updated in 1924 and 1930 from the original design. 'The purpose of this provision was to permit manufacture from this additional coca leaves of a non-narcotic flavoring extract', ensuring destruction of any 'excess alkaloid', 'under the supervision of an authorised representative of the Commissioner'. With no mention of specific interests at stake—Merchandise No. 5 for Coca-Cola—the reports repeatedly stress the rigour of US control routines: ' . . . continuous personal observation of factory operation during the entire process in which these additional supplies of coca leaves are used by a representative of the Commissioner of Narcotics who is furnished samples of all products at various steps in the operation. Labs reported directly to the Commissioner. Not only alkaloid but 'spent leaves themselves, are required to be destroyed by the manufacturers, by *incineration*, and this destruction must take place in the presence of the Commissioner of Narcotics', Harry J. Anslinger. In practice, two representatives—a FBN chemist and 'narcotic inspector', 'were stationed at the factory of this manufacturer [Maywood] to observe and check the . . . process and to witness the destruction', at taxpayers' expense.

The Porter Act of 1930, for which Coca-Cola lobbied (aided by Rep. Stephen G. Porter, chair of the House Foreign Affairs Committee), fortified these procedures. Anslinger immediately granted Maywood rights to purchase 120,000 pounds of 'Peruvian variety' coca for the coming term. Officially designated by the FBN as 'Special' or 'Non-Medicinal' coca leaves, FBN statistics highlight their rising curve from the early 1930s: by

1938, 107,000 kilos of 'non-medicinal' leaf accounted for over half of imported coca, the rest for Merck's cocaine. By the early 1940s, this share rose above 200,000 kilos annually, twice the leaf used for cocaine. Over time official Merchandise No. 5 dwarfed the legal US cocaine-making enterprise. . . .

Coca Diplomacy

Looking ahead to Maywood/Coca-Cola activity—in practice, the two firms became indistinguishable—a kind of political pact congealed with drug officials by the mid-1920s. In the first place, Maywood (and to a lesser extent Merck) embodied the restrictive trade structure that limited import commerce to bulk coca leaf. They provided the Treasury and the FBN access, cooperation and data on every coca-related operation. They enforced the ban on cocaine imports, from which they profited, and naturally vied for a cheap free-trade commerce in leaf with Peru. Maywood employees reported on errant coca sellers or buyers. From 1920 until the 1960s, this cooperation and intelligence-sharing pervades FBN archives. Moreover, Coca-Cola and Maywood used their networks in Peru to gather data coveted by Anslinger (coca crops, legal developments etc.) who became exceedingly knowledgeable about Peruvian cocaine. They exerted informal pressures on the Peruvian state to adopt US-style drug policies. In the pre-1950 era, before the State Department and FBN began to meddle directly in Peruvian drugs (as Peru stayed outside League jurisdiction), such corporate mediation was essential, if not always successful. For example, for US aims and cheap coca, Maywood worked against state monopolies in coca, which Peruvian experts advocated as national drug control. Maywood practiced 'coca diplomacy', manipulating purchases when FBN officers so desired. Coca-Cola lawyers participated in world drug conferences and Andean missions and offered technical advice and political intelligence on evolving coca questions. As Harold Hirsch, famed Coca-Cola vice-president, put it in 1933: '[US] policy . . . has been definitively fixed by the Harrison and Porter Narcotic Acts, and this Company has at all times in good faith cooperated with the Narcotic Bureau of the Treasury and will be pleased to continue to so cooperate with that Bureau and the Department of State both at home and abroad,'

In return, the Anslinger-era FBN paid close attention to Coca-Cola needs. They opposed Peru's statist coca projects, against the thrust of US drug-control philosophy, concerned from the outset with stemming overseas raw material sources. They pressured for cheap leaf. This was vital, for Peru held a de facto world monopoly in extract-leaf (but not cocaine-grade coca, which by the 1910s spread to tropical colonies like Java and Formosa). Peru could have steeply increased the costs of making Coca-Cola, particularly in a world formally set on limiting coca crops. The US government also certified to the world, and its prying drug agencies, that Coca-Cola syrup was definitively not a narcotic substance, a recurring protectionist slogan across the globe even in the 1950s. In sum, the FBN actively aided Coca-Cola's global market conquests. Then as postwar debates intensified on coca's future, the state defined and defended Coca-Cola's long-term interests in international drug treaties, still visible in the 1961 UN Single Convention.

Anslinger also backed Coca-Cola in home markets, helping stifle irksome 'cola' competition. Drug-controllers benefited from a simplified monopoly structure. But dating from the coca-product craze of the 1890s, many firms and individuals had claimed formulas and rights for coca extracts, eager to ply to competing soft-drinks. The FBN worked to keep them out of business, in effect enforcing Coca-Cola's near monopoly. Over time most patent-era cola imitations gave up, a trend broken only by the 1970s by coca-less Pepsi's rise, aided by the Nixon regime. (The great 1980s marketing fiasco of 'New Coke' also revolved around a type of coca-less Coke, though few aficionados realise the meaning of 'classic' in Coca-Cola.) The FBN ensured strategic-goods status for Maywood during World War Two—a dramatic era of Coca-Cola's expansion on the fronts and in global culture. Finally, by the 1960s the United States began to help Coca-Cola prepare for a utopian drug-control era without Andean coca. This has yet to occur, of course, due not only to native Andeans' allegiance to coca culture but to the post-1970s boom in illicit cocaine, which now spreads the coca bush far and wide.

CHAPTER TWO

Exploring Cocaine in the 1960s, '70s, and '80s

Studying the Hot
New Drug:
Unknown Effects

Joel Greenberg

In 1978 Joel Greenberg, former science editor for the *Los Angeles Times*, was a writer at *Science News*. This article about research on cocaine highlights the great degree of ambiguity at the time about the drug. The article opens by recounting the Bourne affair, in which a national drug adviser was found to have used cocaine—but was not dismissed from his position. At this time, the author writes, cocaine was simply not seen as extremely dangerous. Greenberg uses the publication of the first major scientific study of cocaine as an opportunity to examine various cultural aspects of the drug. More important, the author states that very little is actually known about the effects of the drug, negative or positive.

Perhaps the only eyebrows raised over [President Jimmy Carter's advisor on drug policy] Peter Bourne's alleged cocaine use were those within the Carter administration. As an indication of the growing acceptance of coke use, the Bourne episode—during which the deposed White House drug advisor reportedly snorted cocaine through a rolled up currency bill of undisclosed value—was witnessed by one or more *Washington Post* reporters who apparently didn't even think it was worth a story at the time. The item was publicized only when Bourne

---

resigned after admitting he falsified a patient's name on a Quaalude prescription.

If there is any illegal substance that has enjoyed "good press" and comparative public tolerance over the years, it is cocaine. Heroin and other narcotics are seen as killers that at best reduce Human beings to needle-pecked addicts. Marijuana has settled into an era of benign acceptance and in the process appears to have lost some of its mystique. And alcohol, the staple of chemical mind-alterers, is still widely consumed by all classes of people despite its long-acknowledged role as destroyer of livers and exterminator of brain cells.

Cocaine, on the other hand, seems to carry a type of respectability, sophistication and even desirability among drug takers and observers of the "drug scene." Much of the mystique stems from coke's limited supply and high price. The current street price ranges from $60 to $100 a gram. But at least an equal contributor to cocaine's lure is its lore: ". . . the exotic properties attributed to it have contributed to cocaine's street reputation as the status drug," says the National Institute on Drug Abuse's Robert C. Peterson in NIDA's recent research report on the drug.

Among the first to articulate a sense of the cocaine high was Paolo Mantegazza. In his 1859 "The Coca Leaf and Cocaine Papers," Mantegazza reported a rush of "phantasmagoric images" after chewing a quantity of coca leaves. In addition to a doubling of his pulse rate, the scientist described a state of delirium that produced a sensation of flying through colorful visions.

Somewhat of a Mystery

Sigmund Freud was one of many to describe "cocaine bugs," or "the hallucination of small animals moving in the skin." Such visions have been sufficiently realistic in some cases that users have been known to injure their skin in futile attempts to remove the offending coke critters. French researchers have published accounts of one patient who, "scraping his tongue, imagines that he sees small worms coming out of it. . . . The (second patient) tears off his skin and again, looking in the bottom of the wound, pulls out the microbes with his fingernails or with the point of a pin. The third . . . occupies himself with looking for crystals of cocaine under the skin."

Aside from such isolated reports, however, the bulk of cocaine research has yielded little evidence that the drug is dangerous when taken in moderate doses. In the NIDA report—a four-year, $4 million undertaking—Peterson states that "serious adverse effects of use may be quite rare." One reason might be that because coke is so expensive and hard to get relatively few Americans use the drug—and when they do it is in small quantities. Data from several nationwide surveys show that among persons 12 years of age and older, 3 to 4 percent say they have tried cocaine and fewer than 1 percent said they had taken the drug within the month prior to the survey. In the 18- to 25-year-old group, the peak age group for all illicit drug use, 13.4 percent say they have tried cocaine, 2 percent within a month of the survey. Cocaine figures rarely—less than 1 percent of the time—in drug-related emergency room episodes. And in a recent five-year study of drug-related deaths in 27 U.S. and Canadian cities, just 26 involved cocaine alone.

Many of the suspected properties of cocaine—a white, translucent crystalline powder extracted from the coca leaf—remain somewhat of a mystery to scientific investigators. Medically, cocaine has been used as a local anesthetic for many years. And when taken in moderate doses (10 to 25 milligrams intravenously or 100 milligrams intranasally), cocaine appears to significantly increase both heart rate and blood pressure. The NIDA report documents heart rate increases of from 30 to 50 percent and blood pressure jumps of from 10 to 15 percent. A blood vessel constrictor, cocaine when snorted may cause chronic inflammation of the nasal membranes, ulceration and local tissue death. But while perforation of the nasal septum is often mended in anecdotal accounts, "in the United States, at least, this consequence appears to be rare," according to the NIDA study.

Many of the psychic effects of the drug have yet to be confirmed through systematic scientific study. Freud himself, however, has been among those to provide personal, detailed accounts of cocaine's effects on thought and perception. He and others have reported a sense of intense stimulation, psychic and physical well-being and reduced fatigue. Other users have told of tremors, paranoia and a variety of hallucinations.

In addition to the perceived presence of bugs or vermin, reported incidences of hallucination have included seeing things or people that are not present, experiencing vertigo and a "flickering" before the eyes, a general loss of tactile feeling and a sensation of floating on a cushion of air. Some of these hallucinations resulted from chronic use, others only from injection and others from snorting or from chewing a coca leaf.

A Landmark Study

One of the first systematic attempts to study cocaine-induced hallucinations was published in the March [1978] *American Journal of Psychiatry*. University of California at Los Angeles scientist Ronald K. Siegel examined and tested 85 "recreational users" of cocaine who had used at least one gram a month (intranasally) for 12 months. Of those subjects, each of whom underwent visual imagery and a variety of other tests at UCLA'S Neuropsychiatric Institute, 37 experienced some perceptual phenomena—consisting mainly of increased sensitivity to light, halos around bright lights and difficulty in focusing the eyes. . . .

While Siegel's work may represent a significant advance in detailing the hallucinatory effects of cocaine, the question of whether the drug carries any long-term debilitating effects remains unanswered. Although the occurrence of coke hallucinations is frequently referred to as "cocaine psychosis," the UCLA findings do not suggest any severe disturbances of thought or emotion among those who hallucinated. The psychological profiles of those taking part in the study . . . were all essentially normal, according to Siegel. This "would seem to indicate that the reported phenomenology, might simply be an acute pharmacological effect of the drug and not a symptom of incipient psychosis," he says. And anecdotal reports linking cocaine use to aggression and criminality have yet to be validated by research, says NIDA'S Peterson.

Conversely, the alleged positive effects of coke—such as the enhanced endurance, physical strength, creativity and intellectual capacity suggested by Freud and others—also remain unconfirmed by controlled scientific study. Indeed, "much of the anecdotally based information about the drug has never been subjected to systematic investigation," Peterson says.

The Popularity of Cocaine

Lacking hard evidence in either direction, cocaine continues to be, if nothing else, desirable. "Unlike such drugs as LSD and heroin, which are frequently viewed as leading to greater orientation toward self and one's internal processes, cocaine is considered by users as a social drug—one which facilitates social interaction," according to Peterson. "At least part of its appeal is its rarity, high price and use by celebrities, musicians and other folk heroes."

But there is a real, basic quality of appeal that transcends its social status as the "in" drug—namely, the cocaine "high." For many users, the various uncomfortable sensations or hallucinations that the drug may bring are outweighed by its euphoric effect.

In animal studies, where social status and celebrity use exert little force, cocaine is almost uniformly demonstrated to be highly desirable. In one of the latest such studies, rhesus monkeys were allowed to choose (by pressing a lever) between intravenous injections of cocaine and food reinforcement every 15 minutes for eight days. "The animals chose cocaine almost exclusively," Thomas G. Aigner and Robert L. Balster of Virginia Commonwealth University's pharmacology department report in the August 11 [1978] *Science*. The monkeys continued to select coke despite decreased food intake, weight loss and "marked behavioral toxicity," including excessive grooming, scratching, facial grimacing and continuous movement of the head. "All of these exaggerated behaviors disappeared after the study ended," report the researchers. "At no time were any convulsions observed."

These and other animal results might seem to provide a basis for the human theory that, although not physiologically addictive, cocaine may cause "psychological dependence" in some users. "Evidence for the potent positive reinforcing properties of cocaine should be considered in the etiology of recreational cocaine use by humans," say Aigner and Balster.

In the medical environment, the drug is considered valuable in a variety of situations, primarily those requiring anesthesia. Harvard University's Andrew T. Weil has suggested that a coca-based chewing gum could be used as a combination stimulant, antidepressant and antacid. The leaves of the western South American shrub have been chewed by Bolivian and Peruvian Indians since antiquity for religious, medicinal and work-related reasons. The chewing of the coca leaf has supposedly enabled the Indians to work under difficult conditions of high altitude and inadequate diet. Weil's research has determined that the leaves are rich in calcium, iron, phosphorous, riboflavin and vitamins A and E.

The leaf, however, is not nearly so potent—or potentially abusable—as its pure, powdered extract, which experts emphasize can cause death in high-enough concentrations. And whatever the risks and benefits, cocaine appears to be gaining steadily in use and popularity, despite its relative rarity and illegality. But use is still not widespread enough to provide scientists with a large enough sample upon which to conclusively assess the drug's potential.

"Although most cocaine use, even in a social recreational

setting, does not produce adverse medical or psychological consequences, one should not necessarily conclude that cocaine use is harmless," advise David E. Smith and Donald R. Wesson of the Haight-Ashbury Free Medical Clinic and San Francisco Polydrug Research Project. "If the drug were more readily available at a substantially lower cost, or if certain socio-cultural rituals endorsed and supported higher dose patterns, more destructive patterns of abuse could develop."

Coca Versus Cocaine

Andrew Weil

Today, Dr. Andrew Weil is a leading expert on alternative medicine, nutrition, and homeopathic healing. He directs the Program in Integrative Medicine at the University of Arizona in Tucson. But in 1974 Weil was traveling and studying in Colombia and discovering, among other things, the beneficial effects of the coca leaf. In the following account of his journeys, Weil compares the coca leaf and cocaine, arguing that the difference between the two is vast and that equating the two is unfair and inaccurate. Weil advocates for further education of the public about the coca leaf and its benefits and for loosening of restrictions on the import of the plant.

The international arrivals section of Eldorado Airport, Bogotá, Colombia, one night in mid-December of last year. Passengers who have cleared customs enter the long hall of airlines through double doors and are met by porters, friends, and taxi drivers. The author is sitting nearby waiting to meet someone.

Enter through the double doors a man and a woman in their mid-thirties, Americans, non-hippies. The woman wears a long summer dress, the man Bermuda shorts—inappropriate clothes for Bogota's 8,000-foot altitude. They might have just stepped off a plane from Miami. Both of them seem agitated. They look around, not sure where to go. The woman sees the author and walks up to him.

Woman (breathlessly): Excuse me, do you speak English?

Author: Yes.

Woman: Well, we just got off the plane this minute. Can you tell us where we can get some cocaine right away tonight?

When I first came to Bogotá in 1965, Eldorado Airport was less fancy but more hospitable. As soon as passengers cleared customs they were ushered to a round pavilion and served free cups of delicious coffee, compliments of the national coffee-growers association. Today, free samples of cocaine might be more to the point. A great many visitors to Colombia have cocaine uppermost in their minds, and it is said that the amount of money involved in its illegal export to the north makes it at least as important economically as coffee.

It is not surprising that many of the cocaine seekers who come to Colombia are Americans. The popularity of cocaine in our country is at an all-time high. More important, its use has now invaded the world of the middle classes, just as marijuana use began to do a decade ago. One consequence of this change is a growing campaign on the part of middle-class lawyers, doctors, and educators to convince the public in general and judges in particular that cocaine is much less harmful than our laws make it out to be. For example, a number of test cases are now pending in state and federal courts throughout the country that might result in removal of the drug from its usual classification as a narcotic (along with heroin and other opiates) and in a lowering of penalties for its private, recreational use.

The Lure of Cocaine

Many people who try cocaine in our country must wonder why it is so popular. It is a very expensive drug, often selling for as much as $50 a gram or $1,000 an ounce. (The legal retail price in the pharmaceutical trade is $25 an ounce.) Usually, it comes as a crystalline powder in various shades of off-white. Some people shoot it intravenously like heroin, but the vast majority of users snort it. When snuffed up the nose, it very quickly produces a strong sensation of numbness in the nasal passages and throat. Often, American black-market cocaine does little else, and it is curious that people pay so much money to have their noses numbed.

The trouble is that most cocaine is highly adulterated before it reaches the individual consumer—usually with amphetamines, which stimulate by the nasal route as well as by the oral route, and also with procaine and other synthetic local anesthetics that mimic the numbing action of the real stuff. Real cocaine, in addition to its local effects, provides a warm glow of physical and mental well-being, a feeling of energy and clarity without much of the body stimulation of amphetamines or caffeine. But this feeling is subtle and may require learning to perceive. Even with good cocaine, first-time users may not notice that they are high.

What cocaine seems to have going for it mostly is a powerful mystique. It is the rich man's drug, the drug of exotic decadence, a magic tool to prolong and intensify sexual experience. Moreover, the ritual of huddling together to snort precious grains of a forbidden delicacy has a certain romantic charm. . . .

Coca Culture in South America

The coca shrub, *Erythroxylon coca*, is widely cultivated in eastern Peru and Bolivia, its probable area of origin. It grows there in the lush, green valleys of the eastern slopes of the Andes— a region known as the Montaña—often at altitudes well above 5,000 feet. It is also cultivated, though less extensively, in northern Chile, Ecuador, southern Colombia, throughout the Amazon basin, and in many parts of the Old World, principally Java and Ceylon.

I first saw living coca while traveling by car in Bolivia nine years ago. Steep hillsides were planted with the neat shrubs, most of them about three feet tall. And in La Paz, the Bolivian capital, whole sections of the open Indian markets were given over to coca vendors. . . .

The flavor of coca is quite delicious, especially mixed with a bit of *cal, lejía,* or baking soda, all of which add a nice saltiness. Most plants that contain alkaloids are bitter, and many leaves contain astringent tannins, but coca, especially when freshly dried, has a pleasing taste that most people like right from the first. In chewing coca the idea is to build up a chaw of leaves about the size of a walnut and to maintain that between the cheek and gums, letting the juices trickle down the throat. The leaves are not swallowed. After forty-five minutes or so, all the active material is extracted, and one can spit out the remains.

During the time that I stayed in La Paz it was very cold in the mornings, and the lack of hot water where I was living made it an ordeal to get out of bed. I found that a morning chew of coca made it easier to start the day. I had never tried cocaine then and had no particular expectations of the leaves except that I had read a number of testimonials about them. I enjoyed the taste and the novel sensation of numbness in the mouth and throat, but I was disappointed that I did not feel high. At that time I did not realize that the high of coca is subtle, that it requires learning to appreciate, and that [one's psychological] set and setting play a great role in shaping it. . . .

Firsthand reports about Indian uses of coca usually emphasize that regular chewing of the leaf is consistent with good health, high social productivity, and long life. Moreover, much of the literature on coca talks about the therapeutic virtues of the leaf: not only is it not harmful, it is said to provide nourishment for the body and to be useful in the treatment of many kinds of illnesses. On the other hand, some authorities who have no firsthand knowledge of Indians condemn coca chewing as a destructive habit.

To get more information on coca I decided to visit some Indians who use it regularly. I also decided not to do that in the Andes, where cocaine has become so prominent. On the advice of a Colombian botanist friend, I flew from Bogotá to Mitú, the tiny administrative capital of the huge territory of Vaupés, a stretch of the Amazon basin that borders on Brazil. Mitú's main street runs a few blocks from the unpaved airstrip at one edge of town to the bank of the broad Río Vaupés at the other. In Mitú I found two Cubeo Indian boys who took me in a motored canoe up the Vaupés to the Rio Cuduyarí, one of its tributaries, and then up to the Cuduyarí several hours to a tiny village of Cubeos. I was assured that the Cubeos use coca constantly and are amenable to visits. . . .

During the time that I lived with the Cubeos I saw coca used only at the start of communal work parties and at fiestas, when it was consumed in moderation, mainly by men, always accompanied by [cassava] *chicha* and music. Although every house had a supply of prepared coca, I saw no one dip into the supplies except in the company of others for purposes of work or recreation. Young people rarely used it. I took coca almost every day and each time found it tasty and pleasantly stimulating. I developed no craving for it, no desire to increase the dose, and no sense of becoming tolerant to the effect. I saw no evidence among these Indians that coca use was addictive, dependence-producing, or injurious to health. Some old men in the tribe had used coca all their lives and still were satisfied with the occasional consumption of ordinary-size doses.

When I finally left the village to go back to Mitú and then to Bogotá, I carried with me my can of powder and bag of toasted leaves. I was eager to tell people about the virtues I sensed in this plant and to explore its possible uses in modern medicine. . . .

The Benefits of Coca

According to Indian tradition, coca was a gift from heaven to better the lives of people on earth. Over the years South American Indians have found the leaf beneficial in numerous ways. Aside from its ability to clear the mind, elevate mood, and make energy available, it appears to exert good influences on many physical functions. For example, it tones and strengthens the entire digestive tract, probably enhancing the assimilation of foods. A hot-water infusion of coca sweetened with a little raw

sugar (called *agua de coca*) is an excellent remedy for indigestion and stomach-ache that was widely used even by non-
Indians throughout South America until relatively recently.

Coca appears to maintain the teeth and gums in a good
state of health; it keeps teeth white. The leaf is rich in vitamins,
particularly thiamine, riboflavin, and C. An average daily dose
of coca leaves (two ounces) supplies an Indian of the high
sierra with much of his daily vitamin requirement. Coca appears to have a beneficial influence on respiration, and is said
to effect rapid cures of altitude sickness. It also rids the blood
of toxic metabolites, especially uric acid. Indians say that regular use of coca promotes longevity as well.

When European doctors carried coca back to their conti-
nent, they were able to confirm many of the therapeutic powers attributed to it, and prescribed it widely to patients. Propri-
etary tonics based on coca became extremely popular. Our
own Coca-Cola is an emasculated descendant of one of these
nineteenth-century preparations.

My personal experiences with coca leave me convinced
that the leaf is pleasant to consume and moderately stimulating in a useful way. It does not appear to be associated with
dependent behavior or to provoke development of tolerance. It
can be left alone if one chooses.

By contrast, cocaine is much less pleasant to consume, easily becomes associated with dependent behavior, is not very
useful, and is very hard to leave alone. Yet in our society a great
many people are using cocaine, and hardly anyone has seen a
coca leaf. How have we managed to create such a situation?

Drug abuse is much more than the use of illegal and disap-
proved drugs by some members of society. It is the whole
mentality that leads a society to make available to its citizens
worse drugs rather than better ones, and many of us con-
tribute to that mentality. The pharmacologist who teaches that
coca and cocaine are equivalent, the physician who esteems
synthetic white powders above natural green preparations and
the judge who believes that cocaine is used mainly in combi-

nation with heroin are all as much responsible for unwise use of drugs as the user who takes cocaine in excess.

Replacing Cocaine

Throughout all of the argument as to why people use illegal drugs, we sometimes fail to notice the obvious: that people tend to use whatever is available. Over the past eighty years, everything we have done as a society to "protect" people from potentially harmful drugs has served to make worse preparations more and more available. The situation with cocaine is a paradigm of the process.

If a demand for a drug exists, it will be supplied. The demand for cocaine in our country is high, and black-market traffic in it will grow. There is no chance of curtailing the use of cocaine by trying to cut off the flow of it or by punishing users and sellers. But there might be a chance of trying to interest users in coca and thereby encouraging them to shift their attention to something distinctly better.

On returning from the Amazon, I shared my coca with a number of cocaine users. All of them liked it and some said they would like to use it instead of cocaine. Of course, I told them a lot about the leaves in advance so that they chewed them with a good set. Set and setting are especially important in shaping reactions to natural drugs like coca.

Ignorance about coca is widespread. Not only have few cocaine users ever seen a coca leaf, many of them do not even know that coca exists. Some people who have heard of coca confuse it with cacao, the source of chocolate and cocoa. I have met almost no American physicians who are knowledgeable about coca.

I have often written that mental states triggered by drugs are latent in our own nervous systems and may be elicited by a variety of non-pharmacological methods. But I do not think it is reasonable to expect most people to be able to do without pharmacological aids. The use of drugs in our country is very great, and many of the legal ones, such as alcohol, tobacco, coffee, and tranquilizers, cause more social and medical trouble than some of the illegal ones. It is unrealistic to think we can make drugs go away. But we can teach people how to use them in better ways. One step in that kind of education would be to explain that natural drugs are less of a problem than isolated active principles and that certain natural drugs, like coca, are beneficial if used occasionally and with respect for their power.

The Indians I know who use coca respect their drug. They honor Mama Coca by treating her plant reverently, preparing it for use carefully, and guarding its power by saving it for occasions when they need it. The essence of drug abuse is nothing more than failure to honor the wisdom and power of Nature, which has provided us with remedies of great efficacy to sustain us through the toils of day-to-day existence.

Cocaine as a Status Symbol

Jerry Hopkins

Jerry Hopkins worked as a correspondent for *Rolling Stone* magazine for more than twenty years, writing stories about musicians and popular culture. In this article, published in 1975, he takes a detour from the music scene to discuss the growing popularity of cocaine among rock stars and other wealthy elites. The author interviews a wealthy cocaine dealer and describes the popularity of cocaine paraphernalia such as coke spoons and snorting straws in the mainstream. Hopkins also focuses on music and movie references to cocaine. He points out the sale of a drug believed to be cocaine in *Easy Rider* and references to cocaine in lyrics by bands Steppenwolf, the Eagles, and the Who, among many others. By focusing on the saturation of cocaine influence in popular culture, Hopkins demonstrates how cocaine became the "gourmet trip."

In the early 1970s, along with bisexuality, platform heels and *Deep Throat*, cocaine snorting became chic, was in some sub-cultures *de rigeur*, crossing all generation gaps and reaching into Bel Air mansions, Harlem tenements, Berkeley crash pads and split-level rancheros in Middle America with equal facility and dispatch.

There is a story told by Gary Stromberg, who was the Rolling Stones' personal publicist when they toured the U.S. in 1972 and still goes on the road regularly with bands, thus is exposed to a large slice of the popular marketplace. "Do you know how many coke spoons I see and do you know who's wearing them around their necks?" he asks. "Fourteen-year-olds! In Cleveland, man. In Cleveland and Houston and Minneapolis."

Gary says he was startled at first, because as anyone "into it" knows, most people who use it don't wear paraphernalia where every cop in town can see it. More important, in 1974 cocaine was selling for between $1,000 and $2,000 an ounce, $50–$80 for a "spoon" (or gram)—the latter being about enough to get two people high for about half an hour.

"Those kids couldn't have known from cocaine," the publicist says. "But they bought the image, they bought the symbol, they bought the coke spoon, and hung it on a chain with a roach clip, a cross, a Star of David."

A registered pharmacist chuckles when he hears this story. He buys cocaine from the Mallinkrodt Chemical Works in St. Louis, or possibly from the Merck Chemical Company in West Germany, for $22.40 an ounce. And it's pure, while what is sold illegally on the street has been "stepped on," or cut, an unknown number of times with such variant substances as Vitamin B-12 (popular in 1974), methamphetamine (generally agreed to be a bummer) and (the old standby, used for its innocuous taste) a baby laxative called Minite.

Worse, much of the coke being sold is not even cocaine at all, but a mix of procaine and methedrine—procaine being one of several chemical combinations that are more anesthetic than stimulant: thus, the blend with speed. And when it *is* coke, because the drug passes through so many hands on the way to the consumer, the actual cocaine may be reduced to only 6 to 30 per cent of the snort.

Why would anyone pay up to 10,000 per cent mark-up on a product he knows has been brutally adulterated? In the glittery, shattered early '70s, cocaine offered more than chemical euphoria—it also offered a higher station in life. In a word, Status. In a drug-oriented society, coke had become the gourmet trip.

Portrait of a Pusher

Ted is one of the top dealers in New York. He is 24 and black. "Consider the accessories," he says. "Now you can buy a little brass coke spoon tucked inside a 30 caliber bullet for $2.95, add a dollar for a neck-chain, but if you're really into coke, man, you're into fine accessories. You don't put something that expensive in brass. You carry it around in a silver vial— maybe it's even monogrammed. And you snort from a silver spoon. That's my marketplace. I don't sell to the musicians any more. It was far-out being on that scene in a way, but only a few of the musicians have any re-finement, if you know what I mean. My man has to have class. Now I sell on Park Avenue."

Still, gourmet drug or not, much of the traffic of the early '70s is in the low-income or no-income "hip" community. At first it may seem puzzling. Then it becomes clear that many of the coke-heads are dealing, as in the marijuana market, just enough to keep themselves in coke.

"Look," says a smalltime pusher, "I can buy a fairly clean ounce for 1,500 bucks, step on it once and double my money, or sell half after I cut it, get my money back and still have half an ounce for myself."

He pulls a small glass vial of white powder from the pocket of his faded, embroidered, patchwork jeans, carefully sprinkles two thin rows of the powder on a pocket mirror, tightly rolls a new $20 bill, places one end next to one row, the other end in his right nostril. He presses his left nostril closed and inhales through his right, vacuuming the powder in a swift movement along the row. SNIFFFFFFFF. He breathes deeply, then repeats the procedure with the other row and the other nostril. SNIFFFFFFFF.

(Coke can also be dropped, rubbed on the gums, or shoved as a suppository, although these techniques are rarely used, and shot, which is popular largely amongst ghetto blacks and "needle-freaks," and usually thought to be outside the circle of status-heads. Even sprinkling it on an open cut will get the user high. Coke is that readily absorbed.)

Almost immediately the pusher's heartbeat accelerates, his body temperature rises slightly, his pupils dilate, his face flushes a little, his nose numbs. In minutes he will become garrulous, restless, excited. He will feel confident, larger than life.

"Dynamite!" he says, holding the vial aloft. "Wanna little taste? The first snort's on me."

Of course the pusher would like his snorting partner to buy a gram or two. But that does not mean the offer of a free nosefull was necessarily made merely in the interest of salesmanship. The coke may have been offered for other reasons entirely. "Some people," says one Los Angeles user, "don't even do it to get high. It's social now. It's like: 'I've got so much money I can afford to give you some.'" . . .

Rock and Roll Beginnings

In California, much of the hip white establishment was aboard the cocaine train by 1969, when coke made its first important, contemporary film appearance, as record producer Phil Spector made a buy from actors Dennis Hopper and Peter Fonda in *Easy Rider*. At the time, many of the viewers thought the drug Phil was snorting was heroin; never in the film was the drug identified. But neither was the act of snorting *any drug* ever challenged; *no moral judgments were made.* The attitude seemed to be that which Spector himself took the following December when he used a photograph from the film as his Christmas card. There was Phil, one finger held firm against one nostril, snorting a white powder from a tiny spoon through his other nostril. With the message: "A Little Snow At Christmas Time Never Hurt Anyone!"

(Actually, nearly a year ahead of *Easy Rider* came *The Night of the Following Day*, a kidnap-thriller starring Marlon Brando, Richard Boone and Rita Moreno, the latter of whom seemed to spend most of the film snorting coke through a tightly rolled $100 bill. The film was not successful and can be said to have contributed little if anything to "cocaine consciousness.")

By late 1969 the rock and roll rush was on, as dozens of the top stars were known to be using coke regularly. In San Francisco, many of these stars also were including coke references in their new songs. Paul Kantner of Jefferson Airplane, for example, released his first solo album, in it a song called "Hijack," which opened with a simile: "The summer was dry like your nose when you've been behind coke for a day and a season." A year later Paul was back with Grace Slick in another album, *Sunfighter*, which came with a booklet carrying the message, "Those of you who are serious about this whole thing, oozing along like a Cadillac, need some good solid hospital wacco in the nose." While the Grateful Dead (in the summer of 1970) released an album that included a song they played at most concerts, "Casey Jones": "Drivin' that train / High on cocaine / Casey Jones, you better watch your speed." The following year (1971) the Dead returned with a best-selling single, singing about "living on reds, Vitamin C and cocaine" in another concert favorite, "Truckin'."

In Los Angeles, meantime, another rock band, Steppenwolf, had a minor hit the same summer (1971) with a song written by Hoyt Axton, "Snowblind Friend": "He said he wanted Heaven / But prayin' was too slow / So he bought a one-way ticket / On an airline made of snow." Suddenly the word "Cocaine!" made an emphatic appearance between the third and fourth verses of John Lennon's "Hold On John." And then came a blues with a Cole Porter-ish lyric from Taj Mahal: "Champagne don't drive me crazy / Cocaine don't make me lazy / Ain't nobody's business what I do."

The big push came in the late summer of 1972. This was when a Los Angeles band called the Eagles went onto the singles charts with a song called "Witchy Woman." Part of the lyric was coke-inspired—"Crazy laughter in another room / And she drove herself to madness with a silver spoon"—and the record went to No. 9, remaining on the charts for 13 weeks. . . .

By 1973 there was a degree of market saturation that was astonishing. Whirling almost dervishly in its continuing quest for new life styles to exploit, the hungry media settled briefly on that of the black pimp and suddenly there were dozens of magazine articles and books and television reports—most of them featuring cocaine and its use and sale quite prominantly. In head shops, bookstores and boutiques in all major cities and most smaller ones there was a rash of cocaine posters. One had the word "Cocaine" emblazoned across a large red circle in "Coca Cola" script. (This reverse rip-off also appeared on tee-shirts.) Another was a reproduction of one of the soft drink's vintage serving trays, showing the Coca Cola girl lifting a spoon to her nose. (Coca Cola, ever diligent in the protection of registered trade marks—and fragile sensitivities—sued to halt distribution, and won.) While cocaine paraphernalia in stores—spoons, vials, dispensers and snorters—began crowding some of the more traditional marijuana roach clips and hash pipes.

As the popularity of the drug increased, the product proliferated, and as the product proliferated, the popularity of the drug increased.

There was also by now a rapidly developing cocaine "mytholody," the story-telling that made certain dealers, smugglers, events and rituals "legend in their time." There was a dealer from Minnesota, for example, who successfully crossed customs in Los Angeles (coming from Peru) with two kilos of coke taped to his legs and torso by placing a note inside his passport that read: "I'm a federal narcotics officer and am traveling without identification. I'm following the brunette with the big purse. Please expedite my crossing and hers. There could be violence." Another story told often in the rock circuit had the singer of a No. 1 novelty dance record investing the $40,000 he made from his hit in cocaine, then living for four years off the profit of that.

On a recent tour of the English group, the Who, a dealer called "Mr. Peru" appeared backstage in Atlanta and Montreal, and was replaced by "Mr. Bolivia" in Dallas, Detroit, Boston and Philadelphia. In New York there were small devices that looked like a large fat silver bullet with a rod-like handle—hold the rod and turn the bullet and exactly one snort's worth is expelled from the bullet's nose: a steal at $250. While in another area of ritual, it became known that if the user rubbed cocaine onto the glans penis, numbing it, he could prolong his sexual performance indefinitely—or, at least, until the coke ran out.

Before 1974, rock bands had to stock up before leaving their East coast or West coast homes to go on tour, but then coke was available everywhere. Perhaps a little less so in New York, where new laws made dealing so perilous, but according to publicist Gary Stromberg, "it didn't mean coke wasn't available—it only meant it was somewhat harder to find and considerably more expensive."

The rapidly swelling staffs of the U.S. Bureau of Narcotics and Dangerous Drugs in New Orleans, Atlanta and Miami, major ports of entry for illegal cocaine, add further testimony to increased volume. And whereas police in dozens of cities reported few arrests for possession or sale of the drug a few years earlier, by 1974 the arrests and charges were numerous. It was quite clear that the black market for coke was greater than ever before in the drug's 110-year-old history. . . .

Thus, in 1974, cocaine was socially canonized. One could imagine a magazine advertisement with the headline: "What kind of man snorts coke? The man with an expense account. . . ."

Or the man who lived like he had one.

Introducing the National Drug Control Strategy

George H.W. Bush

President George H.W. Bush held office from 1989 to 1993. At the start of his term, he appointed the nation's first drug policy director, William Bennett, and launched a nationwide campaign to fight drugs—specifically, cocaine. Previous president Ronald Reagan had begun this "war on drugs," but Bush made it a cornerstone of his domestic policy agenda. In this national address, the president introduces his new drug control strategy, naming cocaine as his main concern. He deplores the rise of crack in public housing projects, among other issues. Bush's drug control strategy includes stronger enforcement of existing drug laws, increased efforts to combat South American cocaine cartels, and expanded funding for addiction treatment and prevention programs.

Good evening. This is the first time since taking the oath of office that I felt an issue was so important, so threatening, that it warranted talking directly with you, the American people. All of us agree that the gravest domestic threat facing our nation today is drugs. Drugs have strained our faith in our system of justice. Our courts, our prisons, our legal system, are stretched to the breaking point. The social costs of drugs are mounting. In short, drugs are sapping our strength as a nation. Turn on the evening news or pick up the morning paper and you'll see

George H.W. Bush, address to the nation, Washington, DC, September 5, 1989.

what some Americans know just by stepping out their front door: Our most serious problem today is cocaine, and in particular, crack.

Who's responsible? Let me tell you straight out—everyone who uses drugs, everyone who sells drugs, and everyone who looks the other way.

Tonight, I'll tell you how many Americans are using illegal drugs. I will present to you our national strategy to deal with every aspect of this threat. And I will ask you to get involved in what promises to be a very difficult fight.

Crack Is the Problem

This is crack cocaine seized a few days ago by Drug Enforcement agents in a park just across the street from the White House. It could easily have been heroin or PCP. It's as innocent-looking as candy, but it's turning our cities into battle zones, and it's murdering our children. Let there be no mistake: This stuff is poison. Some used to call drugs harmless recreation; they're not. Drugs are a real and terribly dangerous threat to our neighborhoods, our friends, and our families.

No one among us is out of harm's way. When 4-year-olds play in playgrounds strewn with discarded hypodermic needles and crack vials, it breaks my heart. When cocaine, one of the most deadly and addictive illegal drugs, is available to school kids—school kids—it's an outrage. And when hundreds of thousands of babies are born each year to mothers who use drugs—premature babies born desperately sick—then even the most defenseless among us are at risk.

These are the tragedies behind the statistics, but the numbers also have quite a story to tell. Let me share with you the results of the recently completed household survey of the National Institute on Drug Abuse. It compares recent drug use to 3 years ago. It tells us some good news and some very bad news. First, the good. As you can see in the chart, in 1985 the Government estimated that 23 million Americans were using drugs on a "current" basis; that is, at least once in the preceding month. Last year that number fell by more than a third. That means almost 9 million fewer Americans are casual drug users. Good news.

Because we changed our national attitude toward drugs, casual drug use has declined. We have many to thank: our brave law enforcement officers, religious leaders, teachers, community activists, and leaders of business and labor. We should also thank the media for their exhaustive news and editorial coverage and for their air time and space for antidrug messages. And finally, I want to thank President [Reagan] and Mrs. Reagan for their leadership. All of these good people told the truth: that drug use is wrong and dangerous.

But as much comfort as we can draw from these dramatic reductions, there is also bad news, very bad news. Roughly 8 million people have used cocaine in the past year. Almost 1 million of them used it frequently—once a week or more. What this means is that, in spite of the fact that overall cocaine use is down, frequent use has almost doubled in the last few years. And that's why habitual cocaine users, especially crack users, are the most pressing, immediate drug problem.

What, then, is our plan? To begin with, I trust the lesson of experience: No single policy will cut it, no matter how glamorous or magical it may sound. To win the war against addictive drugs like crack will take more than just a Federal strategy: It will take a national strategy, one that reaches into every school, every workplace, involving every family.

Earlier today, I sent this document, our first such national strategy, to the Congress. It was developed with the hard work of our nation's first Drug Policy Director, Bill Bennett. In preparing this plan, we talked with State, local, and community leaders, law enforcement officials, and experts in education, drug prevention, and rehabilitation. We talked with parents and kids. We took a long, hard look at all that the Federal Government has done about drugs in the past—what's worked and, let's be honest, what hasn't. Too often, people in government

And while illegal drug use is found in every community, nowhere is it worse than in our public housing projects. You know, the poor have never had it easy in this world. But in the past, they weren't mugged on the way home from work by crack gangs. And their children didn't have to dodge bullets on the way to school. And that's why I'm targeting $50 million to fight crime in public housing projects—to help restore order and to kick out the dealers for good.

Taking the Fight to South America

The second element of our strategy looks beyond our borders, where the cocaine and crack bought on America's streets is grown and processed. In Colombia alone, cocaine killers have gunned down a leading statesman, murdered almost 200 judges and 7 members of their supreme court. The besieged governments of the drug-producing countries are fighting back, fighting to break the international drug rings. But you and I agree with the courageous President of Colombia, Virgilio Barco, who said that if Americans use cocaine, then Americans are paying for murder. American cocaine users need to understand that our nation has zero tolerance for casual drug use. We have a responsibility not to leave our brave friends in Colombia to fight alone.

The $65 million emergency assistance announced 2 weeks ago was just our first step in assisting the Andean nations in their fight against the cocaine cartels. Colombia has already arrested suppliers, seized tons of cocaine, and confiscated palatial homes of drug lords. But Colombia faces a long, uphill battle, so we must be ready to do more. Our strategy allocates more than a quarter of a billion dollars for next year in military and law enforcement assistance for the three Andean nations of Colombia, Bolivia, and Peru. This will be the first part of a 5-year, $2 billion program to counter the producers, the traffickers, and the smugglers.

I spoke with President Barco just last week, and we hope to

acted as if their part of the problem—whether figh
production or drug smuggling or drug demand—wa:
problem. But turf battles won't win this war; teamwo

Tonight, I'm announcing a strategy that reflects th
nated, cooperative commitment of all our Federal ag
short, this plan is as comprehensive as the problem.
strategy, we now finally have a plan that coordinate
sources, our programs, and the people who run th
weapons in this strategy are the law and criminal jus
tem, our foreign policy, our treatment systems,
schools and drug prevention programs. So, the basic v
we need are the ones we already have. What's been la
a strategy to effectively use them.

Laying Out the Plan

Let me address four of the major elements of our s
First, we are determined to enforce the law, to make our
and neighborhoods safe. So, to start, I'm proposing t
more than double Federal assistance to State and local l.
forcement. Americans have a right to safety in and a
their homes. And we won't have safe neighborhoods
we're tough on drug criminals—much tougher than v
now. Sometimes that means tougher penalties, but more
it just means punishment that is swift and certain. We
heard stories about drug dealers who are caught and ar
again and again but never punished. Well, here the rules
changed: If you sell drugs, you will be caught. And
you're caught, you will be prosecuted. And once you're
victed, you will do time. Caught—prosecuted—punished.

I'm also proposing that we enlarge our criminal justice
tem across the board—at the local, State, and Federal l
alike. We need more prisons, more jails, more courts, n
prosecutors. So, tonight I'm requesting—all together—an
most $1.5 billion increase in drug-related Federal spending
law enforcement.

meet with the leaders of affected countries in an unprecedented drug summit, all to coordinate an interAmerican strategy against the cartels. We will work with our allies and friends, especially our economic summit partners, to do more in the fight against drugs. I'm also asking the Senate to ratify the United Nations antidrug convention concluded last December [1988].

To stop those drugs on the way to America, I propose that we spend more than a billion and a half dollars on interdiction. Greater interagency cooperation, combined with sophisticated intelligence-gathering and Defense Department technology, can help stop drugs at our borders.

And our message to the drug cartels is this: The rules have changed. We will help any government that wants our help. When requested, we will for the first time make available the appropriate resources of America's Armed Forces. We will intensify our efforts against drug smugglers on the high seas, in international airspace, and at our borders. We will stop the flow of chemicals from the United States used to process drugs. We will pursue and enforce international agreements to track drug money to the front men and financiers. And then we will handcuff these money launderers and jail them, just like any street dealer. And for the drug kingpins: the death penalty.

Treatment and Prevention

The third part of our strategy concerns drug treatment. Experts believe that there are 2 million American drug users who may be able to get off drugs with proper treatment, but right now only 40 percent of them are actually getting help. This is simply not good enough. Many people who need treatment won't seek it on their own, and some who do seek it are put on a waiting list. Most programs were set up to deal with heroin addicts, but today the major problem is cocaine users. It's time we expand our treatment systems and do a better job of providing services to those who need them.

And so, tonight I'm proposing an increase of $321 million

in Federal spending on drug treatment. With this strategy, we will do more. We will work with the States. We will encourage employers to establish employee assistance programs to cope with drug use; and because addiction is such a cruel inheritance, we will intensify our search for ways to help expectant mothers who use drugs.

Fourth, we must stop illegal drug use before it starts. Unfortunately, it begins early—for many kids, before their teens. But it doesn't start the way you might think, from a dealer or an addict hanging around a school playground. More often, our kids first get their drugs free, from friends or even from older brothers or sisters. Peer pressure spreads drug use; peer pressure can help stop it. I am proposing a quarter-of-a-billion-dollar increase in Federal funds for school and community prevention programs that help young people and adults reject enticements to try drugs. And I'm proposing something else. Every school, college, and university, and every workplace must adopt tough but fair policies about drug use by students and employees. And those that will not adopt such policies will not get Federal funds—period!

The private sector also has an important role to play. I spoke with a businessman named Jim Burke who said he was haunted by the thought—a nightmare, really—that somewhere in America, at any given moment, there is a teenage girl who should be in school instead of giving birth to a child addicted to cocaine. So, Jim did something. He led an antidrug partnership, financed by private funds, to work with advertisers and media firms. Their partnership is now determined to work with our strategy by generating educational messages worth a million dollars a day every day for the next 3 years—a billion dollars' worth of advertising, all to promote the antidrug message.

The Need for Support

As President, one of my first missions is to keep the national focus on our offensive against drugs. And so, next week I will take the antidrug message to the classrooms of America in a special television address, one that I hope will reach every school, every young American. But drug education doesn't begin in class or on TV. It must begin at home and in the neighborhood. Parents and families must set the first example of a drug-free life. And when families are broken, caring friends and neighbors must step in.

These are the most important elements in our strategy to fight drugs. They are all designed to reinforce one another, to mesh into a powerful whole, to mount an aggressive attack on the problem from every angle. This is the first time in the history of our country that we truly have a comprehensive strategy. As you can tell, such an approach will not come cheaply. Last February I asked for a $700 million increase in the drug budget for the coming year.

And now, over the past 6 months of careful study, we have found an immediate need for another billion and a half dollars. With this added $2.2 billion, our 1990 drug budget totals almost $8 billion, the largest increase in history. We need this program fully implemented—right away. The next fiscal year begins just 26 days from now. So, tonight I'm asking the Congress, which has helped us formulate this strategy, to help us move it forward immediately. We can pay for this fight against drugs without raising taxes or adding to the budget deficit. We have submitted our plan to Congress that shows just how to fund it within the limits of our bipartisan budget agreement.

Now, I know some will still say that we're not spending enough money, but those who judge our strategy only by its price tag simply don't understand the problem. Let's face it, we've all seen in the past that money alone won't solve our toughest problems. To be strong and efficient, our strategy needs these funds. But there is no match for a united America, a determined America, an angry America. Our outrage against drugs unites us, brings us together behind this one plan of action—an assault on every front.

This is the toughest domestic challenge we've faced in

decades. And it's a challenge we must face not as Democrats or Republicans, liberals or conservatives, but as Americans. The key is a coordinated, united effort. We've responded faithfully to the request of the Congress to produce our nation's first national drug strategy. I'll be looking to the Democratic majority and our Republicans in Congress for leadership and bipartisan support. And our citizens deserve cooperation, not competition; a national effort, not a partisan bidding war. To start, Congress needs not only to act on this national drug strategy but also to act on our crime package announced last May, a package to toughen sentences, beef up law enforcement, and build new prison space for 24,000 inmates.

The Nation Must Unite

You and I both know the Federal Government can't do it alone. The States need to match tougher Federal laws with tougher laws of their own: stiffer bail, probation, parole, and sentencing. And we need your help. If people you know are users, help them—help them get off drugs. If you're a parent, talk to your kids about drugs—tonight. Call your local drug prevention program; be a Big Brother or Sister to a child in need; pitch in with your local Neighborhood Watch program. Whether you give your time or talent, everyone counts: every employer who bans drugs from the workplace; every school that's tough on drug use; every neighborhood in which drugs are not welcome; and most important, every one of you who refuses to look the other way. Every one of you counts. Of course, victory will take hard work and time, but together we will win. Too many young lives are at stake.

Not long ago, I read a newspaper story about a little boy named Dooney who, until recently, lived in a crack house in a suburb of Washington, DC. In Dooney's neighborhood, children don't flinch at the sound of gunfire. And when they play, they pretend to sell to each other small white rocks that they call crack. Life at home was so cruel that Dooney begged his teachers to let him sleep on the floor at school. And when asked about his future, 6-year-old Dooney answers, "I don't want to sell drugs, but I'll probably have to."

Well, Dooney does not have to sell drugs. No child in America should have to live like this. Together as a people we can save these kids. We've already transformed a national attitude of tolerance into one of condemnation. But the war on drugs will be hard-won, neighborhood by neighborhood, block by block, child by child.

If we fight this war as a divided nation, then the war is lost. But if we face this evil as a nation united, this will be nothing but a handful of useless chemicals. Victory—victory over drugs —is our cause, a just cause. And with your help, we are going to win.

Thank you, God bless you, and good night.

Cocaine Policy in the 1980s

Jefferson Morley

Jefferson Morley has been writing about the state of the nation and the world for over thirty years. Currently, he writes the World Opinion Round-Up column in the *Washington Post*. In the following article, excerpted from the October 2, 1989, issue of the *Nation*, Morley leads the reader through a general overview of cocaine drug policy from the 1960s and 1970s before launching into a scathing attack on the U.S. "war on drugs." According to Morley, the cocaine trade in the United States is a fine example of capitalism at work, and then-President George H.W. Bush's drug strategy only encouraged the development of a healthy, market-driven cocaine industry.

It was in July 1969 that President Richard Nixon called for a "new urgency and concerted national policy" in the fight against drugs. But for the Vietnam War, drugs might then have been regarded as a national crisis. Two decades later we have a fresh urgency, George Bush's newly announced national strategy, and no colonial war to distract us. There is civil strife in Colombia and vague talk of having U.S. troops put the entrepreneurs of Medellín and Cali in their place. There is a drug czar, our homegrown version of Gen. Wojciech Jaruzelski, who actually said earlier this summer, "A massive wave of arrests is a top priority for the war on drugs." And three cocaine kingpins now rank among the planet's wealthiest human beings. Twenty years of war on drugs have coincided with the emergence of a vast and sometimes frightening international cocaine economy.

Drug czar William Bennett and President Bush propose abolishing the cocaine economy altogether. Never known for their antipathy to capitalism, they nonetheless call for the annihilation of one of its highest-growth sectors, the drug business. Bennett and Bush aspire to rid us once and for all of this allegedly immoral marketplace and its amoral entrepreneurs. Or do they?

The history of the cocaine economy is not reassuring. Its growth can be divided into three periods. In each, leading drug enforcers have, wittingly or unwittingly, reached forms of de facto accommodation with leading drug dealers.

The first period witnessed the birth of the cocaine economy, between 1969 and 1974; during that time, new state regulations gave decided commercial advantage to cocaine smugglers. The second period was the cocaine boom, which lasted from 1975 through 1982; in it, the executive branch launched a serious, coordinated, high-level effort to prosecute drug bankers—and then abandoned it. The third was the consolidation period, which began in 1983 and continues to this day; the burden of the war on drugs has been shifted onto the producing nations, onto the crack economy and onto the casual users—and away from the North American elite of the trade. A fourth period may yet be defined by Bennett and Bush. In foreign policy, the President and the drug czar want expanded powers to attack the insurgent capitalists at home in Latin America. In domestic policy, they want expanded powers to discourage consumption and petty entrepreneurship in drugs. The cocaine economy has become a central part of American political culture.

Pioneers of Reaganism

Nixon's war on drugs hastened the professionalization of the drug commerce. Between 1969 and 1974, surveillance of the

Mexican border was increased and Mexican marijuana fields were sprayed with paraquat, a herbicide. Amateur smugglers were driven out of the drug business. "In their stead more professional groups flourished," observes sociologist Patricia Adler of the University of Colorado at Boulder, who wrote *Wheeling and Dealing*, a study of a fluid circle of successful drug entrepreneurs in southern California. These professional groups were made up of "people who could rise to the new sophistication demanded by the law enforcement challenge and who could afford the technology and equipment capable of avoiding detection."

By treating marijuana and cocaine as equally dangerous, Nixon's drug war stimulated the cocaine economy. Cocaine powder is more easily transported and concealed than bulk marijuana, insuring both less risk and higher profit. Undifferentiated prohibition of cocaine and marijuana gave a competitive advantage to the more compact—and physiologically hazardous—drug. Between 1974 and 1980 Adler saw the transformation of San Diego from "a major wholesale marijuana market into a distribution center for the cocaine trade." Dozens of other North American cities underwent a similar transformation in the same period.

A new capitalist elite was taking shape at the top of the drug economy: The producers and exporters were increasingly Colombian, while Americans in the top echelon assumed roles as domestic wholesalers, bankers, pilots and money launderers.

The market advantage of cocaine did not, of course, create the demand for the drug that drove the boom of the late 1970s. Demand probably created supply more than vice versa. Cocaine, a brisk euphoriant, was the ideal drug for millions of people coping with rapid economic change. With the first oil shock of 1973, the fortunes of the poor and the middle class began to erode. Manufacturing industries were giving way to service and information firms, especially in the cities. "The metaphoric associations of cocaine are those most in line with an acceptance of economic and cultural life under capitalism," one critic of the Miami vice noted, for "no other drug works as well: Heroin becomes too debilitating . . . while marijuana has too many passive associations—one cannot be 'laid back' in the 'fast lane.'" Cocaine was the drug for those who were getting ahead—and for those who could only dream of getting ahead.

The drug counterculture of the 1960s, with its emphasis on LSD and marijuana, had been eclipsed. The cocaine entrepreneurs stood at the center of the new culture of pleasurable consumption. They had "abandoned their predominantly instrumental, goal-seeking, controlled, and future-oriented behavior" for a more pleasure-oriented, sexually permissive livelihood, according to Adler. In this respect the marketers of cocaine are heirs to the drug counterculture of the 1960s. But if upwardly mobile drug entrepreneurs shared countercultural impulses, they were also fully imbued with the values of consumer capitalism. "Rather than seeking out antimaterialist, sixties style communes," Adler notes, "these people retained (even intensified) the value of materialism which pervades our society." They were, in her analysis, irrational materialists, hedonists addicted to profit and recklessness.

In retrospect, they look like nothing so much as the pioneers of Reaganism.

Operation Greenback

The cocaine boom of the late 1970s generated a tremendous cash bonanza for the rising elite of North American drug entrepreneurs. Bankers were needed in Miami to handle the cash, and there was little difficulty enlisting them.

The best available index of the dollar volume of the drug trade is the statistic on currency flow kept by the Federal Reserve Board. Every bank turns its cash deposits over to the local Federal Reserve branch office. A currency surplus results when all the banks in a Federal Reserve district receive more cash than they pay out. In most areas of the country, deposits and payouts are roughly balanced. In Florida in the late 1970s, bankers were taking in cash by the duffel bag from you know who. The currency surplus in Florida was $576 million in 1970; by 1976 it had almost tripled, to $1.5 billion.

Officials in the enforcement section of the Treasury Department "detected the surplus and connected it to the large scale laundering of drug receipts" in 1976, according to a high-level Treasury Department brief obtained under the Freedom of Information Act. "Detailed information was brought to the attention of DEA and the Criminal Division of the Department of Justice," the report says. Despite the "detailed" evidence, no concerted action was taken against drug bankers between 1976 and 1979.

Only after *Parade* magazine and *60 Minutes* did exposés on respectable drug profiteers in 1979 did the Feds finally launch Operation Greenback. That interagency task force, which consisted of representatives from the Federal Reserve, the Treasury Department and the Justice Department, was the Federal government's first (and some would say last) serious national effort to curb drug banking.

Operation Greenback enjoyed some success in its early years, but its overall failure is instructive. It was taking on an enormous challenge, both practically and politically. A 1982 money-laundering investigation disclosed that one suburban branch office of Capital Bank in Miami had accepted $242 million in drug-tainted cash in less than eighteen months. If the cash surplus is a rough indicator of the volume of the drug trade, that was something like 5 percent of the cash in the flourishing Florida drug trade—a big cut, to be sure. But it would have taken at least thirty comparable money-laundering operations—and as many bankers—to generate the whole cash surplus in the state of Florida. In fact, when analysts from Operation Greenback began examining financial reports of Miami banks for telltale signs of money laundering, they found no less than twenty-four banks that merited closer scrutiny.

Within two years Operation Greenback was in deep trouble. "There are problems in South Florida that are unhealthy and could be fatal to the Project," one Treasury Department agent reported in June 1982, according to Operation Greenback documents. Chief among them was what one Greenback prosecutor delicately called "the procedures under which cases are selected for investigation."

Operation Greenback had collided with the institutional interests of the banking industry. In May 1982, William von Raab, U.S. Customs Commissioner, attended the annual meeting of the Florida Bankers Association and scolded the "sleazy institutions who are intentionally profiting from this dirty business." One banker shouted, "You are using us as a whipping boy," and the furious financiers immediately adjourned the meeting. Another problem was that Federal Reserve Bank examiners were not trained in, and therefore not interested in, tracking money laundering, according to former U.S. prosecutor Richard Gregorie. And yet a third hindrance was that the Reagan Administration was easing rather than tightening the regulation of financial institutions. Reagan's hiring freeze limited the number of bank examiners and Internal Revenue Service agents available to pore over financial records and look for things like savings and loan fraud and money laundering. Both flourished.

George [H.W.] Bush, appointed to lead the nation's antidrug efforts in March 1982, "wasn't really too interested in financial prosecution," says Charles Blau, the chief prosecutor in Operation Greenback at the time. Within a year of Bush's appointment, Greenback was downgraded from a senior interagency committee in Washington to a unit within the office of the U.S. Attorney in Miami. Meanwhile, the cash surplus in the cities of Jacksonville and Miami had risen to $5.2 billion.

The best that can be said for the scaled-back version of Operation Greenback is that it seems to have forced drug financiers to move their operations to California. The Justice Department attributes the unprecedented $3 billion cash surplus that developed in southern California in 1988 to increased money-laundering operations in Los Angeles. But the State

Department's biannual narcotics report notes that the "emerging group of professional, criminal financial managers" doesn't need greenbacks in sacks anymore. Drug banking is now done mostly through electronic transfers, the report says. The entrepreneur's duffel bags full of cash are "not laundered or otherwise converted, but simply held against future need."

U.S. District Court Judge Peter Beer, who heard the money-laundering case involving Capital Bank, noted how natural it is for the discreet banker to launder drug money. "With only a little softening of traditional concepts of business mortality and the violation of a few somewhat obscure federal statutes," Beer observed in his 1982 decision, "a 'fee' hungry bank could be (and in this case became) an ideal laundry system. No one needed to get really involved. It would only be necessary that no one be too inquisitive." Few in the Bush Administration are inquisitive about drug banking.

In fact, prosecution of drug bankers is a very low priority in Bush's so-called national strategy. Operation Greenback is defunct and the once-tiny Capital Bank has since expanded its operations to Washington, D.C. The bank that collected a quarter-billion dollars in drug receipts in 1980–81 now has a gleaming branch office two blocks from George Bush's White House

The New Entrepreneurs

Entrepreneurs in the crack trade are not so well situated. They too belong to a growth industry, but the urban crack market is fraught with fierce competition for scarce profits and scarcer social respect. Again, the economic transformations of the 1970s are crucial. Economic institutions withdrew from the poor urban (and rural) communities, where much of the crack commerce takes place. Urban areas lost entry-level jobs, especially in blue-collar industries. The new jobs that were created there required higher levels of education, but the quality of education in urban black communities could not keep up. The drug economy increasingly became the major cash-generating commerce in the areas abandoned by global capitalism.

By the mid-1980s the cocaine market was consolidating and prices were dropping. "As classically happens in cases of market saturation," says Terry Williams, author of *Cocaine Kids*, "a new product was introduced which offered the chance to expand the market in ways never before possible. Crack, packaged in small quantities and sold for $5 and sometimes even less—a fraction of the usual minimum sale for powder—allowed dealers to attract an entirely new class of consumers." It also created a whole new class of entrepreneurs: African-American teen-agers, who need little startup capital and who reject traditional authority.

The urban drug entrepreneur is portrayed as a member of "the underclass" and the victim of the so-called culture of poverty. Yet, according to diverse media accounts, the crack entrepreneurs often display those traits purportedly absent from said culture: work discipline, personal abstention from the drug abuse, and thrift. Crack entrepreneurs do not entirely reject mainstream culture. Like Adler's post-hippie proto-yuppies hanging out in the disco bars of San Diego in the late 1970s, young black entrepreneurs are irrational materialists. Their rebellion is part of their conformism to the larger culture. They spurn the injunctions of parents, police, teachers and other authorities, but they embrace the entrepreneurial and consumption cultures of mainstream America. They are exemplars of the culture of capitalism.

Democratic capitalism sustains no other growth industry in the inner city besides crack. Many white-run businesses have shut down or left for lower costs in the suburbs and overseas. Ethnic petty entrepreneurs, like Korean and Chinese grocers, naturally favor employing their own. Larger firms seem resistant to hiring blacks either because of racist policies or because urban blacks lack the necessary job skills. And during the past fifteen years the Federal government has generally preferred to use transfer payments or trickle-down economics to sustain the ghettos.

The black authority figures who might harness the entre-preneurial zeal of black youth are prone to work in the public sector or in integrated businesses. In either case, they lack the control of capital necessary to employ black youth and build black economic institutions.

So what's a young, gifted and black entrepreneur supposed to do, as a rational economic actor in a capitalist society? "It's a question I hate," Peter Reuter, an economist at the Rand Cor-poration, says, "But a lot of time he or she's going to go into dealing drugs. It is clearly a way for a lot of people in the ghetto to get ahead, at least temporarily and, many times, for longer. For many people it's clearly the only shot they've got for getting out of the ghetto. That said, I think the risk of vio-lence is large, especially in crack, and I don't think you can stay in the trade for an unlimited time without experiencing that violence at some point."

As Williams puts it, "Drugs are the nexus between the cul-ture of refusal and economic opportunity."

CHAPTER THREE

Crack: The Other Cocaine

Understanding Crack: The Scientific Perspective

Dan Waldorf, Craig Reinarman, and Sheigla Murphy

Scientists Dan Waldorf, Craig Reinarman, and Sheigla Murphy began studying cocaine users in 1973 and received a grant in 1986 from the National Institute on Drug Abuse to study cocaine cessation. Their book *Cocaine Changes* is a result of that study. The following excerpt is taken from the chapter on crack use. The authors describe the rise of smokable cocaine and "freebasing," the precursors to crack cocaine, and provide an overview of the effects, chemical composition, and methods of using crack cocaine.

The origins of crack use lie in freebasing, a mode of cocaine ingestion that begins with the processing of cocaine hydrochloride (HCL) or powder to extract a purer, more solid form of cocaine for smoking, which provides a powerful high. Some researchers say the process spread from the coca-producing regions of Peru and Bolivia. Since the mid-1970s South American drug researchers have reported people smoking a partially refined coca paste called *basuco* or mixing this paste with tobacco or marijuana in the form of cigarettes called *pitillos* or *papilloes* (Siegel, 1982). This practice reportedly found its way along smuggling routes to the Caribbean and eventually into the United States via Florida (Inciardi, 1987).

Others say that U.S. cocaine dealers discovered the process in the course of testing the purity of powder cocaine by "basing it down," or heating it in a solution of water, ammonia, and ether to get cocaine base. If, after cuts and impurities had been removed, the remainder, or the return, was 80 to 85 percent of the original weight, the product was considered pure. The resulting base crystals could not be snorted or injected, and dealers did not want to waste them. The long-standing practice of dipping the ends of cigarettes in cocaine powder gave them the idea of smoking the leftovers from their purity tests (McDonnell, Irwin, and Rosenbaum, 1990). No doubt there are other pieces of this history, and competing accounts may not be mutually exclusive.

If the cocaine HCL is heated in a water solution with ammonia and ether, the results are crystalline flakes of cocaine base that are free of impurities and other residual salts and solids used in processing coca paste; hence the term "freebase.". . . If cocaine powder is instead "cooked" in a bicarbonate of soda solution, the result is a solid chunk or "rock," which tends to make a crackling sound when burned; hence the term "crack.". . . Processing by the bicarbonate of soda method does not purify the drug the same way the ether method does; many impurities remain but the cocaine is still in a form that burns more easily than powder cocaine. In either case the resulting product is heated in a pipe until it vaporizes. These vapors are then inhaled by the user.

Freebase Evolves into Crack

The rather fine distinction between freebase and crack is often a confusing one. A long-term snorter and small-time dealer who once experimented with freebase told us that the difference between freebasing and crack use was like "the difference between preparing a gourmet meal and going out to McDonald's." Other respondents agreed. Freebasers usually took pains to prepare their own pure base from relatively large quantities of cocaine powder. It was prepared and used in private homes. The crack that is sold on the street, on the other hand, is typically precooked by dealers in mass quantities in a solution unknown to the user; often cut, prepackaged in smaller units; and frequently smoked in public places.

Freebasing has become almost identical to crack smoking, but this was not always so. In the mid- to late 1970s, when many of our subjects [studied by the authors] began to employ this mode of ingestion, ammonia and ether were used in the extraction process. Although the ether method yielded a pure base that was said to be a cleaner, somewhat stronger high than that now offered by crack, ether was both troublesome to use and dangerously flammable, as Americans learned when comedian Richard Pryor experienced near-fatal burns while using the ether method.

By the early 1980s many freebasers, including most of those in our sample, had switched from ether to the simpler, safer method of cooking that used only bicarbonate of soda and water. This baking soda method yields a less pure, yet still solid form of cocaine suitable for smoking, which is virtually the same as what we now know as crack. With the baking soda method now nearly universal, the current differences between freebase and crack inhere only in who makes it and how it is sold. If made by a dealer rather than by the user, crack can contain more adulterants; and retail dealers tend to sell crack in small, inexpensive units often on street corners and out of crack houses. Thus, although most of our respondents who employed this mode of ingestion used the term "freebase," they now agree that what they are smoking is the same as crack. We will therefore use the terms interchangeably.

Crack Use Increases

Although this form of ingestion is referred to as smoking, which it closely resembles, it is really the inhalation of the vapors ("the cloud") rather than any residual smoke that provides the intense "rush" reported by freebasers and crack smokers. The high from "basing" and crack smoking is said to be far more fast-acting and intense than the high from snorting because relatively pure cocaine vapors are absorbed directly into the bloodstream through the vascular bed of the lung rather than powder being absorbed slowly through the nasal membrane. Thus, higher concentrations of cocaine reach the brain all at once in a matter of seconds rather than a little at a time over a longer period.

A sizable albeit unknown proportion of America's cocaine users began freebasing in the late 1970s or early 1980s (Siegel, 1982). Yet the now ubiquitous term "crack" (or, in San Francisco and Los Angeles, "rock," "work," or "hubba") had not then entered the lexicon (Inciardi, 1987). Crack became recognized as a public problem only in spring 1986 when politicians and the mass media jumped on it as if it were an end-zone fumble.

Although then unknown outside of a few neighborhoods in a handful of major cities, crack caught popular attention for two reasons. First, although freebasing had been around for a number of years, by 1985 dealers had begun to sell smaller, cheaper units of this precooked cocaine base on ghetto street corners. They sold to the increasingly impoverished youth of the black and Latino underclass, many of whom soon became involved in these sales as a faster and arguably effective means of moving out of poverty toward the American dream. Thus crack was cast as a great threat in part because it became associated with a class that was already perceived as "dangerous" (Reinarman and Levine, 1989; see also Duster, 1970). In addition to this shift in the class and racial composition of cocaine smokers (e.g., Washton and Gold, 1987), a growing number of clinical reports claimed that, compared to cocaine powder for intranasal use, this form of cocaine was more "instantly addicting" and more devastating in its consequences.

Crack Starts Its Rise

Jacob V. Lamar Jr.

In the 1980s crack was a very new drug, as this 1986 article by *Time* magazine staff writer Jacob V. Lamar Jr. demonstrates. The nation needed to be educated about crack, the writer feels, and its qualities and dangers. Lamar takes the reader through a brief description and history of the drug before exploring the existence of crackhouses, the physical dangers of crack addiction, and the crime and other ill effects crack was beginning to have on the African American communities in America's inner cities.

In New York City, the sleazy dealers peddling dope in Manhattan's Washington Heights call it "crack." In the south central part of Los Angeles, the desperate addicts chasing an ever more elusive high know it as "rock." On both counts, and in Chicago, Detroit and other cities throughout the U.S., the drug by either name is an inexpensive yet highly potent, highly addictive form of cocaine that is rapidly becoming a scourge. Pushers sell pellet-size "rocks" in tiny plastic vials for as little as $10. Smoked rather than snorted, a single hit of crack provides an intense, wrenching rush in a matter of seconds. "It goes straight to the head. It's immediate speed," says a former addict. "It feels like the top of your head is going to blow off."

In minutes the flash high is followed by a crashing low that can leave a user craving another hit. But that evanescent electric jolt, priced so that almost anyone can afford it, has made crack the drug of the moment. The National Cocaine Hotline estimates that 1 million Americans in 25 states around the country have tried crack. From January through April, while

New York City police seizures of marijuana fell off 92% from the year before and heroin seizures fell off 88%, cocaine seizures rose 41%. Crack busts already constitute 55% of all cocaine arrests in New York. In Los Angeles, where the drug was introduced around 1981, more than two-thirds of the 2,500 coke arrests made this year have involved rock.

The rapid spread of crack leads some experts to fear a new wave of cocaine addiction in the U.S., possibly as serious as the devastation wrought by the heroin wave of the late 1960s. Says Dr. Arnold Washton, director of research for the National Cocaine Hotline: "Last May I had never heard of crack. Today we get nearly 700 to 900 calls a day from people having problems with the drug." Crack is more addictive than any other form of cocaine, says Washton. "It's the dealer's dream and the user's nightmare."

The drug is most popular in the inner city; a recent survey by the cocaine hotline indicates that most abusers are men between the ages of 20 and 35, and that more than half the nation's so-called crackheads are black. In some instances, say experts, heroin addicts have turned to the seemingly safer method of smoking cocaine because of the spread of AIDS among needle-using junkies; some of the needy, smoke-filled "base houses" where crack is sold and consumed were formerly shooting galleries for heroin. But crack's low cost has also made it particularly appealing to adolescents. Kids as young as twelve have called the coke hotline in desperation.

Crack Compared to Cocaine

Cocaine addiction is nothing new in the U.S. According to the National Institute on Drug Abuse [NIDA], some 5 million Americans are regular coke users. But the traditional, sniffed "nose candy" is no match for crack. NIDA estimates that an addiction to regular coke develops after three to four years, while crack abusers are usually hooked after only six to ten weeks. A snort of classic coke penetrates the mucous membrane slowly, circulating to the brain in about eight minutes and producing a high, much milder than crack's, that lasts for 20 minutes or so. Crack is absorbed rapidly through the lungs and hits the brain within seconds in a dangerous, concentrated form.

Using crack is easier and less complicated than free-basing cocaine. Since powdered coke cannot be ignited and smoked, free-basers wash a cocaine base with ether to clean out impurities. Once dried, the residue is heated with a torch and smoked. The extreme volatility of ether makes this a dangerous way to get high—as the general public learned in 1980 when comedian Richard Pryor set himself on fire while free-basing.

By contrast, the process used to make crack is simple. Ordinary coke is mixed with baking soda and water into a solution that is then heated in a pot. This material, somewhat purer and more concentrated than regular cocaine, is dried and broken into tiny chunks that dealers sell as crack rocks. The little pellets are usually smoked in glass pipes. "Crack is a whole new ball game," says James Hall, executive director of Up Front, a Miami drug-information center. "It's an extremely compulsive drug, much more so than regular cocaine. The rush is so intense and the crash so powerful that it keeps users—even first-time users—focused on nothing but their next hit."

Rise in Crime

Police in Florida have noticed increases in burglaries and armed robberies in areas where crack is sold. Says Captain Robert Lamont of the Dade County police narcotics division: "These are the crimes that can generate enough cash for a quick fix. Then it's off to the streets to raise more cash." But robbery is not the only price society pays for crack; the state of near psychosis that heavy cocaine use produces leads easily to violence. New York City police have attributed a recent rash of brutal crimes to young addicts virtually deranged by the new drug. According to Inspector William Molinari of the N.Y.P.D.'s narcotics division, there have been seven crack-related homicides in the city this month. In one instance, police say, Victor Aponte, a 16-year-old addict, confessed to stabbing his mother to death after she caught him smoking crack.

Some cities around the country are beginning to wage all-out assaults on the crack trade. Last week, after local and federal authorities nabbed 44 suspected dealers, New York City Police Commissioner Benjamin Ward announced the formation of a special anti-crack unit, composed of 101 veteran undercover officers. The unit is the first New York police squad ever devoted to fighting a single drug. Miami's 16-month-old street narcotics operation busted seven crack base houses, arrested 485 dopers and confiscated more than $8,000 in cash during a six-week period this spring.

But crackdowns have not slowed the spread of the drug. In Los Angeles, raids by narcotics squads helped reduce the number of "rock houses" from 1,000 in 1984 to about 400 today. The business has merely moved to the streets. Teenage salesmen with rock hidden in their pockets—or sometimes their mouths—now loiter at corners and against fences. As buyers drive by slowly in cars, a quick exchange of cash for crack can take place through an open window.

In the ghettos, the economics of crack has created a lucrative cottage industry. Organized crime has not yet taken over the trade, police believe. Instead, a small-time dealer in Los Angeles can buy an ounce of cocaine for $1,000 to $1,500. Since each ounce contains 28 grams and each gram can produce up to six rocks that he can sell for as much as $25 each, the dealer can realize a profit of around $2,700.

Crack Houses

As local drug entrepreneurs battle it out for dominance, a hierarchy of rock cocaine is being built on violence. In lucrative rock markets like Los Angeles, most dealers' base houses are veritable fortresses, guarded by thugs armed with pistols and sawed-off shotguns. Metal bars cover the windows; steel mesh and heavy beams are used to bar the doors. With some places reaping monthly profits of more than $30,000, dealers need such heavy security to ward off not only cops but competitors.

One rock house busted in south-central Los Angeles looked perfectly innocuous on the outside: a white stucco duplex with a neatly trimmed lawn. Inside, a hallway leading to a bedroom had been walled off. Behind the barrier, a surveillance camera was trained on customers in the living room. The drug salesman, sitting in the kitchen equipped with three telephones and a box full of cash, remained unseen behind a fortified door but was able to monitor the outer room via closed-circuit TV. Buyers spoke to the seller through an intercom. Money and drugs were passed through a tiny opening in the wall.

Some base houses serve as modern-day opium dens, where addicts not only purchase crack but rent pipes, hang out and get wasted. Most of these establishments are run-down and filthy, littered with ragged furniture, trash and graffiti. Rockheads will sometimes stay for days, spending whatever cash they have, so wired from hit after hit that they have no need for food or sleep. Women who run out of money sometimes turn into "cocaine whores," selling themselves to anyone who will provide more crack.

"Eva" is a 16-year-old patient at New York City's Phoenix House drug rehabilitation center who got hooked on crack two years ago. The product of a troubled middle-class family, she was already a heavy drinker and pot smoker when she was introduced to coke by her older brother, a young dope pusher. "When you take the first toke on a crack pipe, you get on top of the world," she says.

She first started stealing from family and friends to support her habit. She soon turned to prostitution and went through two abortions before she was 16. "I didn't give a damn about protecting myself," she said. "I just wanted to get high. Fear of pregnancy didn't even cross my mind when I hit the sack with someone for drugs."

Eva's story is becoming all too familiar in cocaine-treatment centers around the nation. In the popular imagination, cocaine has long had an almost glamorous aura about it: the champagne of drugs, a high for the upwardly mobile who use rolled-up $100 bills to snort lines of expensive white powder. Crack, by comparison, is so inexpensive that it is proving to be an equal-opportunity narcotic, one that does not discriminate among its victims.

Cocaine Sentencing Policy: Crack Versus Powder

Ted Gest

Ted Gest currently heads the program on crime policy and the media at the University of Pennsylvania. In this 1995 article, written when Gest was on staff at *U.S. News & World Report*, he provides a brief history of the controversy surrounding cocaine sentencing policy. Users of crack, mainly African Americans, receive much stiffer penalties, on average, than users of powder cocaine, who are mainly whites. Gest explains that disparities in sentencing laws were set in 1986, in the wake of the violence surrounding the trade in crack cocaine and the high-profile cocaine overdose of basketball star Len Bias. By 1990, he writes, lawmakers were beginning to question whether the disparities were racist.

It's 1986. A new, potent form of cocaine called crack engulfs Florida like wildfire and threatens other regions. Congress, rushing to enact a tough anticrime law before the fall election, establishes a punishment for selling the drug that amounts to a 100-to-1 increase over the penalty for selling it in powder form.

It's 1995. Blacks are serving most of the 5- and 10-year prison terms the law requires. Critics denounce the statute as racist. Jesse Jackson speaks out at demonstrations, but Congress votes down a change. Disturbances break out in four federal prisons, causing inmates nationwide to be locked in their cells.

This is a study in hastily passed legislation with unintended effects. Crack was a huge problem in mid-1980s America—and still is in many communities today. But lawmakers groping for a way to deal with it had no clue that their solution would provoke a storm of controversy over race and crime. Here's how it happened:

In early 1986, with illegal narcotics use rising, a House subcommittee headed by then Representative William Hughes of New Jersey began a review of antidrug laws to ensure that prosecutors and agents had sufficient legal tools. "We wanted the Drug Enforcement Administration to go after high-level traffickers," recalls Eric Sterling, then a Hughes aide. "So we proposed to give them a carrot: higher penalties."

Crack cocaine was a special case. Produced by dissolving powder cocaine in a solution of water and sodium bicarbonate and then boiling it and cutting it into "rocks," crack became the street drug of choice in many areas during the 1980s because it gave users a more intense "high." It was also much cheaper on the street than powder cocaine—selling for between $5 and $20 per rock.

Experts still debate how much more dangerous and addictive crack may be than its powder counterpart, but there is little doubt that it is more associated with street violence. As the drug's popularity increased, so did warfare among dealers. That led to soaring murder rates—and increasing urgency on Capitol Hill.

Lawmakers believed that crack was worse than powder, but the question remained how high to ratchet up the penalty. What followed was a bipartisan exercise in one-upmanship. Bob Dole, then in his first stint as Senate majority leader, proposed a plan from the Reagan White House that would have established a 20-to-1 ratio, meaning that it would take a quantity of crack one twentieth the amount of powder to trigger maximum prison terms of five or 10 years, depending on whether a trafficker was classified "major" or "serious."

The subcommittee was scheduled to meet one day in June 1986 when, an aide recalled, an "ashen-faced [Representative] Dan Lungren walked in and announced that Len Bias had died." The case caused a sensation: The University of Maryland basketball star had succumbed to cocaine intoxication two days after he was drafted by the National Basketball Association. Based on a medical examiner's speculation, Bias was linked to crack in no fewer than 74 segments on the national network news in July 1986. A year later, it turned out that he had snorted powder cocaine and had not smoked crack, but the early media coverage set the tone. In any event, the House upped the ratio to 50 to 1.

Cracking Down

After that, several senators, including Dole, then Judiciary Chairman Strom Thurmond and Democrats Joseph Biden and Lawton Chiles, talked about getting even tougher. Chiles, now governor of Florida, had met with citizens of Florida sheriffs who were alarmed at the damage the drug had done in their counties. Even before Bias's death, Chiles was telling colleagues that crack was horrible.

As the fall of 1986 approached and lawmakers were anxious to adjourn for the election campaign, the two chambers settled on the 100-to-1 ratio. Two years later, in another election-year blitz, Congress applied the mandatory crack penalties to possession cases. Many activists now contend it is a racist law that unfairly targets poor black crack users while the white suburban users of the pricier powder cocaine get lesser penalties. But no one can recall any opposition from sources that are now outraged about the differential, including the Congressional Black Caucus. "Crack was so new [in 1986] and there were no data, so it wasn't debated in racial terms," says a caucus member's aide who worked on the bill. Many members of the black caucus voted for the bills that contained harsher penalties.

By 1990, it was clear that whatever their intent, the anti-crack laws were having a disproportionate effect on African-Americans. The Minnesota Supreme Court ruled in 1991 that a state law treating crack more harshly than powder cocaine unlawfully discriminated against blacks. Several federal trial judges have issued similar rulings, but no appellate court has agreed. Meanwhile, the U.S. Sentencing Commission, a federal panel overseeing crime penalties, says that blacks account for 88.3 percent of crack-distribution convictions. Federal surveys show that a majority of Americans using crack are white. One element in the disparity is that blacks are likelier to be arrested for street deals like those whites may make in suburban homes.

The outlook is murky. Last spring, the federal sentencing panel voted 4 to 3 for equalizing crack and powder penalties, but Congress voted down the plan this fall and asked for more study. . . . Attorney General Janet Reno said that terms for possession should be equalized. Florida Representative Clay Shaw, who proposed the higher sentences, argues that crack remains "out of control" but agrees that the possession issue "deserves a second look." As for trafficking, one politically salable answer may be to raise the penalty for powder and reduce the ratio to 20 to 1—the same idea that Reagan proposed nearly a decade ago.

Editor's Note: To date, discrepancies in sentencing for possession of powder cocaine versus crack cocaine remain controversial.

Crack Culture in East Harlem

Philippe Bourgois

Philippe Bourgois is an associate professor of anthropology at San Francisco State University. While researching his book *In Search of Respect*, he lived with Puerto Rican crack dealers in their neighborhood in East Harlem for five years. In this excerpt from his ethnographic study of poverty, crime, and drug addiction, Bourgois offers a detailed portrait of the crack "economy" in the neighborhood, which provides an income to many dealers even as residents cope with deteriorating infrastructure, used drug paraphernalia littering the streets, and underground "clinics" dispensing remedies to crack addicts. The author also suggests that self-isolation by the residents of "El Barrio" contributes to the lack of a legitimate economy; because residents do not feel connected to the rest of American society, they do not venture outside the inner city.

I was forced into crack against my will. When I first moved to East Harlem—"El Barrio"—as a newlywed in the spring of 1985, I was looking for an inexpensive New York City apartment from which I could write a book on the experience of poverty and ethnic segregation in the heart of one of the most expensive cities in the world. On the level of theory, I was interested in the political economy of inner-city street culture. From a personal, political perspective, I wanted to probe the Achilles heel of the richest industrialized nation in the world by documenting how it imposes racial segregation and eco-

Philippe Bourgois, *In Search of Respect: Selling Crack in El Barrio*. New York: Cambridge University Press, 1995. Copyright © 1995 by Cambridge University Press. Reproduced by permission.

nomic marginalization on so many of its Latino/a and African-American citizens.

I thought the drug world was going to be only one of the many themes I would explore. My original subject was the entire underground (untaxed) economy, from curbside car repairing and baby-sitting, to unlicensed off-track betting and drug dealing. I had never even heard of crack when I first arrived in the neighborhood—no one knew about this particular substance yet, because this brittle compound of cocaine and baking soda processed into efficiently smokable pellets was not yet available as a mass-marketed product. By the end of the year, however, most of my friends, neighbors, and acquaintances had been swept into the multibillion-dollar crack cyclone: selling it, smoking it, fretting over it.

I followed them, and I watched the murder rate in the projects opposite my crumbling tenement apartment spiral into one of the highest in Manhattan. The sidewalk in front of the burned-out abandoned building and the rubbish-strewn vacant lot flanking each side of my tenement began to crunch with the sound of empty crack vials underfoot. Almost a decade later, despite the debates of the "drug experts" over whether or not the United States faces a severe "drug problem," this same sidewalk continues to be littered with drug paraphernalia. The only difference in the mid-1990s is that used hypodermic needles lie alongside spent crack vials in the gutter. Heroin has rejoined crack and cocaine as a primary drug of choice available in the inner city as international suppliers of heroin have regained their lost market share of substance abuse by lowering their prices and increasing the quality of their product. . . .

Crack World Economies

Cocaine and crack, in particular during the mid-1980s and through the early 1990s, followed by heroin in the mid-1990s, have been the fastest growing—if not the only—equal opportunity employers of men in Harlem. Retail drug sales easily outcompete other income-generating opportunities, whether legal or illegal.

The street in front of my tenement was not atypical, and within a two-block radius I could—and still can, as of this final draft—obtain heroin, crack, powder cocaine, hypodermic needles, methadone, Valium, angel dust, marijuana, mescaline, bootleg alcohol, and tobacco. Within one hundred yards of my stoop there were three competing crackhouses selling vials at two, three, and five dollars. Just a few blocks farther down, in one of several local "pill mills," a doctor wrote $3.9 million worth of Medicaid prescriptions in only one year, receiving nearly $1 million for his services. Ninety-four percent of his "medicines" were on the Department of Social Services' list of frequently abused prescription drugs. Most of these pills were retailed on the corner or resold in bulk discounts to pharmacies. Right on my block, on the second floor above the crackhouse where I spent much of my free time at night, another filthy clinic dispensed sedatives and opiates to flocks of emaciated addicts who waited in decrepit huddles for the nurse to raise the clinic's unidentified metal gates and tape a handwritten cardboard DOCTOR IS IN sign to the linoleum-covered window. I never found out the volume of this clinic's business because it was never raided by the authorities. In the projects opposite this same pill mill, however, the New York City Housing Authority police arrested a fifty-five-year-old mother and her twenty-two- and sixteen-year-old daughters while they were "bagging" twenty-one pounds of cocaine into $10 quarter-gram "jumbo" vials of adulterated product worth over $1 million on the street. The police found $25,000 cash in small-denomination bills in this same apartment.

In other words, millions of dollars of business takes place within a stone's throw of the youths growing up in East Harlem tenements and housing projects. Why should these young men and women take the subway to work minimum wage jobs—or even double minimum wage jobs—in downtown offices when they can usually earn more, at least in the short run, by selling drugs on the street corner in front of their apartment or school yard? . . .

Crack World Culture

The anguish of growing up poor in the richest city in the world is compounded by the cultural assault that El Barrio youths often face when they venture out of their neighborhood. This has spawned what I call "inner-city street culture": a complex and conflictual web of beliefs, symbols, modes of interaction, values, and ideologies that have emerged in opposition to exclusion from mainstream society. Street culture offers an alternative forum for autonomous personal dignity. In the particular case of the United States, the concentration of socially marginalized populations into politically and ecologically isolated inner-city enclaves has fomented an especially explosive cultural creativity that is in defiance of racism and economic marginalization. This "street culture of resistance" is not a coherent, conscious universe of political opposition but, rather, a spontaneous set of rebellious practices that in the long term have emerged as an oppositional style. Ironically, mainstream society through fashion, music, film, and television eventually recuperates and commercializes many of these oppositional street styles, recycling them as pop culture. In fact, some of the most basic linguistic expressions for self-esteem in middle-class America, such as being "cool," "square," or "hip," were coined on inner-city streets.

Purveying for substance use and abuse provides the material base for contemporary street culture, rendering it even more powerfully appealing than it has been in previous generations. Illegal enterprise, however, embroils most of its participants in lifestyles of violence, substance abuse, and internalized rage. Contradictorily, therefore, the street culture of resistance is predicated on the destruction of its participants and the community harboring them. In other words, although street culture emerges out of a personal search for dignity and a rejection of racism and subjugation, it ultimately becomes an active agent in personal degradation and community ruin.

As already noted, it is impossible to calculate with any ac-

 THE HISTORY 🍃 OF DRUGS

Monologue: Benzie Speaks

In this portion from Philippe Bourgois's book In Search of Respect, *Benzie, a longtime crack user and dealer, talks angrily about feeling trapped by the drug. His strong feelings are evident in his disjointed and emotional words.*

Benzie: The best way to be, is legal. Survive. Make your money and make everybody love you [opening a ten-dollar packet of heroin and handing me a quart of malt liquor to open].

I want you to be like that, Primo. I've been doing it a year, Primo. Look at this box [holding out a small plastic object], look what it says here. One year, this is a tie rack, this is a tack that goes on a tie. But it's because I've made a year. That's what it says there.

Do you know why I've made a year at this place? [sniffing heroin] Because I've been through f——— coke; [pointing to the cocaine Primo was crushing into sniffable powder in a folded dollar bill] I've been through f——— crack; I've been through marijuana; I've been through f——— every drug. I always was troubulated. But now I'm finally getting mines—my *capacidad* [self-worth]—I've finally got to that stage that I won't do something. [pointing again to the cocaine] I'm tired of f——— crack living. [waving his arm at the vials littering the stairway] Serious, man.

Like right now [pausing to sniff cocaine] I do not do drugs. F——— ! Look at my face. [moving it aggressively to within an inch of mine and taking the malt liquor bottle] I got a round face. When you do drugs you could tell by someone's face. [sniffing delicately from the packet of heroin, using Primo's key as a dipper].

Philippe Bourgois, *In Search of Respect: Selling Crack in El Barrio.* New York: Cambridge University Press, 1995, pp. 95–96.

curacy what proportion of the population is involved in the untaxed, underground economy. It is even harder to guess the number of people who use or sell drugs. Most of El Barrio's residents have nothing to do with drugs. The problem, however, is that this law-abiding majority has lost control of public space. Regardless of their absolute numbers, or relative proportions, hardworking, drug-free Harlemites have been pushed onto the defensive. Most of them live in fear, or even in contempt, of their neighborhood. Worried mothers and fathers maintain their children locked inside their apartments in determined attempts to keep street culture out. They hope someday to be able to move out of the neighborhood.

Understanding the Dealers

The drug dealers . . . consequently represent only a small minority of East Harlem residents, but they have managed to set the tone for public life. They force local residents, especially women and the elderly, to fear being assaulted or mugged. The sight of emaciated addicts congregating visibly on street corners provokes pity, sadness, and anger among the majority of East Harlemites who do not use drugs. Most important, on a daily basis, the street-level drug dealers offer a persuasive, even if violent and self-destructive, alternative lifestyle to the youths growing up around them.

No matter how marginal they may be in absolute numbers, the people who are carving out hegemony on inner-city streets cannot be ignored; they need to be understood. For this reason, I chose addicts, thieves, and dealers to be my best friends and acquaintances during the years I lived in El Barrio. The pathos of the U.S. inner city is most clearly manifested within the street dealing world. To borrow the cliché, "in the extraordinary we can see the ordinary." The extreme—perhaps caricatural—responses to poverty and segregation that the dealers and addicts represent, afford insight into processes that may be experienced in one form or another by major sectors of any vulnerable population experiencing rapid structural change in the context of political and ideological oppression. There is nothing exceptional about the Puerto Rican experience in New York, except that the human costs of immigration and poverty have been rendered more clearly visible by the extent and rapidity with which the United States colonized and disarticulated Puerto Rico's economy and polity. On the contrary, if anything is extraordinary about the Puerto Rican experience, it is that Puerto Rican cultural forms have continued to expand and reinvent themselves in the lives of second- and third-generation immigrants around a consistent theme of dignity and autonomy.

CHAPTER FOUR

Current Issues and Controversies

Cocaine: Still Popular, Still Dangerous

Rebecca Oppenheim

Rebecca Oppenheim writes extensively about health issues in the United Kingdom. In this article, she offers a British perspective on the cocaine problem among youth. Oppenheim writes that cocaine is again on the rise as a party drug, considered safer than Ecstasy or other psychedelics. Young, affluent professionals treat cocaine as a social stimulant, she writes, reserving use for after work and on the weekends. Clearly, though, Oppenheim considers cocaine a dangerous scourge that exposes users to the risk of overdose, heart attack, stroke, and addiction.

Cocaine use in the UK is on the rise, according to the results of the British Crime Survey. Experts are unsure why, but one probable reason is because it has become cheaper. Although prices vary widely across the country, in some areas, such as Leeds, a gram of cocaine can cost as little as 20–25 pounds [about 36–45 American dollars], according to Brendan Cox from UK drug charity DrugScope.

Another possible reason for the increase in cocaine use is the negative publicity surrounding Ecstasy. Annabel Boys, a research psychologist at the National Addiction Centre, in London, has conducted a study into cocaine use and found that attitudes towards certain drugs are changing.

"There was some suggestion that users, particularly younger ones, saw cocaine as less dangerous than Ecstasy and amphetamine," she says. "This was possibly stimulated by the fact that there had been at that time a lot of deaths related to Ecstasy use that had received a great deal of media coverage."

Dangerous Misconceptions

But it's dangerous to think of cocaine as "safer" than Ecstasy, says Brendan. The drug can make users feel alert, energetic and confident. But it can also lead to sweating, loss of appetite and increased heart rate. At higher doses users may feel anxious and panicky. Large doses or quickly repeated doses over a period of hours can lead to extreme anxiety, paranoia and even hallucinations.

Frequent use of the drug or taking it in large doses can also result in serious health problems and, in some cases, death. Approximately 15–20 people in the UK die each year from cocaine overdoses, and figures by researchers at St George's Medical School in south London show that the number of cocaine-related deaths increased by 16 per cent in 2000.

Extensive studies have highlighted the damaging effects of the drug, which include increased risk of heart attack and stroke. Other research suggests cocaine can hamper brain-power manual dexterity for up to a month after the drug is last taken. It is also thought to pose dangers to unborn children if taken by pregnant women.

One US study by researchers at Hennepin County Medical Center in Minneapolis showed that cocaine users were at risk of developing potentially fatal arterial aneurysms. An aneurysm happens when the wall of an artery balloons out under pressure. If it happens in a heart or brain artery, and goes on to burst, it can trigger either a heart attack or stroke.

The study of 112 cocaine users showed that almost one in three had aneurysms in a heart artery—the normal rate in patients with heart symptoms is around 5 per cent.

The drug can also have a neurological effect. Researchers at the US National Institute on Drug Abuse found that cocaine impairs brainpower—particularly among those taking at least 2 grams a week. They say the study adds to a growing body of evidence suggesting that drug abuse can cause long-term problems well after the user has stopped taking the substance.

In addition to the dangers it poses on its own, mixing cocaine with other drugs can bring added problems, says Brendan. If combined with other stimulants such as Ecstasy or speed, it can increase the heart rate to a worrying level.

Annabel's research found that many cocaine users drank alcohol at the same time. This is risky because, whereas cocaine is a stimulant, alcohol is a depressant, so combining the two can have unpredictable effects.

"Light" users of cocaine may experience relatively few long-term health consequences, according to Brendan, although other experts say the lasting effects are not yet known.

The Potential for Addiction

One of the main dangers is the potential for addiction. "Psychological dependence doesn't happen through just one use, it probably takes two to three months to build up that sort of dependency," says Brendan. "But if that does happen, the effects on your lifestyle can be severe because, although cocaine has come down in price, it is still an expensive drug compared to, for example, alcohol."

But despite the risks, there are always going to be some people who continue to use the drug. Pete, 28, is an IT consultant from London. He's been using cocaine for three years, but he cut down when he got worried about becoming dependent.

"Before, it used to give me a massive buzz, like I was 10-foot high and bullet-proof, but the more I did, the more it was like I was maintaining an equilibrium. That's when I started cutting back on it," he said.

Pete sets himself strict limits to make sure his use of cocaine doesn't spiral out of control. "I never do it during the week and try to keep it to less than once a fortnight (fourteen days). It's important to limit yourself otherwise you'd be up for days and just ruin the next week or so," he says.

However, many tabloids suggest cocaine is the celebrity drug of choice. Numerous TV stars have been "caught in the act" and there is a general acceptance in the media, which make some people question whether the drug is still actually illegal.

However, the law is clear about the drug's legal status. As a class A substance, cocaine dealers can be sent to prison for life and users can face a seven-year sentence for personal possession.

The Beat Goes On:
The U.S. War on Coca

Linda Farthing and Kathryn Ledebur

Writers Linda Farthing and Kathryn Ledebur work on the Andean Information Network at the Washington Office on Latin
America, a nongovernmental organization. In the following
article they discuss the conflict between U.S. cocaine policy
and South American coca culture. U.S. cocaine policy, they explain, puts pressure on South American countries to eradicate
coca crops, but efforts to destroy the crops have met with sus-
tained resistance in countries like Bolivia, where coca has been
legally grown and consumed for centuries. Farthing and Ledebur provide both a broad history of the U.S. government's
efforts to eradicate coca in Bolivia since 1980 and an analysis
of the current situation. Since the beginning of the eradication
program, they write, obstacles have been rampant. The authors are critical of the United States, stating that it has failed
in establishing alternative crops for farmers and has ignored
the needs of the Bolivian people.

In unguarded moments during the month-long road blockade
of September and October 2000, coca growers and Bolivian security forces chatted, played soccer and ate together while
they waited for government orders to reinitiate their confronta-
tion. In a country where coca leaves have been legally consumed and used in rituals for centuries—even soldiers chew
the leaf during coca eradication missions and clashes with
protesters—this strangely amicable standoff demonstrates

how, to many Bolivians, U.S. drug control objectives are an external imposition doing more harm than good. A 1998 survey found that even among the military, 73% of personnel believed the armed forces participate in anti-drug efforts as a result of U.S. pressure. "The reality is that the military" commented an ex-officer, "is conscious that eradication has created economic and social conflict."

Just four days after President Carlos Mesa's inauguration in October 2003, U.S. drug czar John Walters warned that "hitching Bolivia's future to coca cultivation could relegate it to permanent backwater status." Mesa soon confirmed the continuation of coca eradication as official state policy. Like presidents before him, Mesa recognized that his country's dependence on international aid forces it to comply with U.S. anti-drug goals despite the social costs. Mesa told the *Wall Street Journal*, "Coca production has fallen, but Bolivia's income has fallen as well, and we haven't received the equivalent compensation."

Ironically, heavy U.S. government pressure has increased popular support for the growers' leader, Evo Morales, and has helped make the Bush administration's concerns about the coca growers' political influence a reality. Recognizing the adverse impact of their remarks, U.S. officials have recently become less vocal regarding Morales and the growers' increasing political clout. U.S. Ambassador to Bolivia David Greenlee echoed Washington's underlying position in May 2004: "I don't talk about Evo [Morales] in public, people really look for the U.S. to demonize him and then support for him goes up. . . . The guy is a kind of godfather of coca in the Chapare . . . and I'm not going to deal with a godfather."

Tensions Mount

Since the mid-1980s, U.S. drug control policy has been largely directed at the Chapare region east of Cochabamba where most of Bolivia's coca leaf destined for transformation into cocaine is grown. The emphasis has always been on violent intervention by special police and military units, rather than the economic assistance programs called "alternative development."

Considering the country holds the world record for coups d'état, it is understandable that most Bolivians are leery of military involvement in domestic affairs. Still, U.S. policy has consistently forced the country's presidents to accept some U.S. and domestic military participation in the "drug war," without regard for the congressional approval required by Bolivian law. Washington has been unwilling to back down despite the conflict generated by its policies and the tremendous cost to Bolivia's sovereignty and stability.

Former dictator Hugo Bánzer, elected president in 1997, established the armed forces as the centerpiece of his anti-drug strategy. Since then, increased responsibility for internal law enforcement—beginning with counternarcotics missions and expanding into other areas—paired with the militarization of the anti-drug police, UMOPAR, has provoked conflict and heightened the traditional rivalry between these forces and Bolivia's national police. Competition for anti-drug resources from the United States has exacerbated the situation. These tensions, coupled with limited respect for democracy and human rights among the security forces, partly contributed to a shootout between the military and the police in February 2003 in front of the presidential palace in La Paz, leaving 33 dead. Indeed, Bolivia's growing unrest and instability are in no small measure due to U.S. drug war policies.

In 1988, the Bolivian government passed Law 1008, a draconian anti-drug law developed by the U.S. government. It provided the justification and framework for the U.S. "war on drugs" in Bolivia and delineated which coca in what areas would be slated for eradication. The implementation of the law has been especially harmful to coca-growing families and those occupying the lower rungs of the cocaine industry, while having little lasting impact on high-level trafficking. Security forces often direct their actions at the easily accessible plots of vulnerable coca-growing families, resulting in human rights abuses and harassment. Recent modifications to Law 1008, however, have addressed some of the most egregious abuses, particularly a number related to constitutional violations and due process. Before the reforms, for example, arbitrary arrest and lengthy incarceration without trial meant that people lacking the means to bribe their way out of jail spent several years in prison without the opportunity to prove their innocence or be sentenced.

Struggling to Find a Balance

Bolivia's other main coca-growing zone is east of La Paz in the Yungas region. The Yungas, however, has only experienced one incursion by military eradication forces—albeit a failed one—and an ineffectual ongoing voluntary eradication program. Eradication efforts have almost exclusively focused on the Chapare, because the government sanctions the 12,000 hectares (1 hectare = 2.5 acres) of coca grown in the Yungas as "legal" and "traditional" whereas the bulk of illegal coca has historically been grown in the Chapare. But with the drop in coca production in the Chapare, Washington has placed greater focus on what it considers the Yungas' burgeoning excess coca crop.

As eradication forces eliminate their principal source of income, farmers have frequently pinned their hopes on the promise of alternative development. Consequently, there is hardly a farmer in the Chapare who has not participated in one of the four major alternative development projects the U.S. government has financed over the past 20 years at a cost of about $270 million dollars. Despite the significant international funding to the region, the vast majority of Chapare residents continue to live at subsistence levels.

Early development programs in the Chapare sought to directly substitute the coca-cocaine economy with other crops, but eventually administrators realized no other crop could directly compete with coca. In the late 1980s, they changed strategy and tried to curb the migration of impoverished Bolivians to the Chapare. During the past 10 years, they have focused on promoting the cultivation and export of bananas, passion fruit, hearts of palm, black pepper and pineapple. Eradication of coca has always been a condition for participation in these programs, and U.S. policymakers generally per-

 THE HISTORY OF DRUGS

The *Cocaleros'* Perspective

Writing in March 2003, journalist Reed Lindsay describes the devastating effect that U.S.-led coca-eradication programs have had on one Bolivian farmer and his family.

For more than a month, some 200 Bolivian soldiers have been living and defecating in Victor Franco's backyard.

The soldiers, trained and financed by the United States to eradicate coca in this jungle river basin, arrived in helicopters, setting up camp a stone's throw from Franco's house, a dirt-floored structure made of unevenly cut wooden planks and a rusted sheet-metal roof.

They pitched tents on top of his small yucca plantation and chopped down his pineapple plants and mandarin tree to clear a helicopter landing pad.

At first, they left Franco's coca plants alone, instead eradicating the crops of other families in the area. Twice, soldiers came to Franco asking for a small amount of coca, a mild stimulant that is a staple among Bolivia's rural poor and indigenous people.

Then, within a few days of harvest, the soldiers chopped down their host's coca plants.

It was the fourth time his crop has been eradicated, says Franco, 42, his cheek bulging with coca leaves as he squats with family and neighbours in the shade of a mango tree.

"How can they cut down all our plants?" sobs his wife, Gomercinda Franco, in her native language of Quechua, wiping away tears with her arm. "I have eight children. What are we going to live on? All our coca is gone."

Reed Lindsay, "Coca Growers Fight Back," *Toronto Star*, March 16, 2003.

ceived this conditionality as the key to success. Whereas good economic development practice considers the participation of strong local organizations an enormous asset, in the Chapare, the U.S. Agency for International Development (USAID) has consistently demonized the tight-knit campesino unions—the principal representatives of the growers—calling their members and leaders "drug traffickers."

Added to these two elements—exclusion of local representatives and conditionality—is the enormous challenge of conducting development programs in a zone of recurring conflict. After 20 years of unfulfilled promises, coca-growing families are deeply distrustful of the United States and are not likely to differentiate between U.S.-funded military and police actions and U.S.-funded development programs. In fact, official U.S. documents rarely make this distinction; almost every government publication on alternative development makes it clear that coca eradication and not economic development is the primary goal in the Chapare. Indeed, alternative development serves as a political tool in the war on drugs, attempting to put a friendlier face on a repressive policy designed to separate campesinos from their livelihoods without providing viable alternatives.

U.S. Leadership

Both of these poorly formulated facets of the U.S. war on drugs—militaristic intervention and alternative development— saw their maximum expression in Plan Dignidad (Plan Dignity), the forced eradication program initiated in 1998 to curry favor with the U.S. Embassy. Bánzer used the military to eradicate a record 45,000 hectares of coca—most of the Chapare's production—by 2000. Touted by U.S. officials as a huge victory, accelerated forced eradication steeply increased human rights violations and contributed to one of the country's worst economic crises. Forced eradication also strengthened opposition to other U.S.-backed policies promoting economic liberalization, such as the privatization of basic services and natural resources.

Washington dictates how the war on drugs will be fought in Bolivia and controls the purse strings. In the Chapare, the U.S. government trains, equips and funds all anti-drug units, providing even the salary bonuses for anti-narcotics police, military eradication officials and prosecutors. Since the implementation of Plan Dignidad, the U.S. government has paid for and supervised the construction and expansion of military and police installations throughout the region, despite an October 2000 agreement between the Bolivian government and coca growers prohibiting the building of new bases. U.S. government agencies, such as the Drug Enforcement Administration (DEA) and the Narcotics Affairs Section (NAS) of the embassy, share a base with local anti-drug forces in Chimore and closely supervise the Bolivian units' operations. Control is so tight that Bolivian eradication commanders must obtain embassy permission for each flight in helicopters donated and fueled by the U.S. government. . . .

In spring 2003, attempts by the U.S. Embassy to link Bolivian coca growers to leftist Colombian guerrilla groups became explicit. U.S. officials continue to publicly express concerns about what they call "narcoterrorism" in the Chapare, providing additional justification for militarization. Although security force commanders in the region cite the increased sophistication of exploding booby traps, they do not accuse terrorists of operating in the region. In 2003 and 2004 district attorneys filed terrorism charges against more than 100 Chapare coca growers. Prosecutors have not presented compelling evidence, and some has clearly been fabricated. Six of those charged are still in jail and none of the cases have come to trial.

The first three months of the Mesa administration were peaceful in much of the country, but in the Chapare, three security officers were killed. In apparent retaliation, the armed forces burned the homes of 25 coca growers and tortured three coca growers detained on terrorism charges. Calm returned during the first half of 2004, largely as a result of the growers' strategic focus on the December 2004 municipal elections and their decision to give the Mesa administration some breathing room. The destruction of a key bridge by floodwaters effectively blocked the highway for four months, providing a de facto road blockade that limited access for eradication missions. Yet the underlying problems in the Chapare remain unresolved, as the basic policy of militarized eradication without sufficient economic alternatives is unchanged.

In the absence of significant income from alternative development, producers have quickly replanted in the Chapare and coca production has increased in the Yungas region as well. In March 2004, the U.S. State Department reported that Yungas coca production rose by 26% and that nationwide production rose 17% beyond 2002 estimates. Resistance to drug war policies is growing concomitantly with the crops in the Yungas. Well aware of the consequences of U.S. policy in the Chapare, coca growers blocked the sole road into the Yungas, as their counterparts had done in the Chapare, for three days to protest the U.S.-financed construction of a drug control base at La Rinconada. Although the Mesa administration initially agreed to halt construction, it changed its stance a week later, citing heavy pressure from the U.S. Embassy . . .

Looking Ahead

Promised changes are slow in coming. Coca growers began vigils around eradication camps last September, protesting the failure to implement the proposed alternative development strategy. Confrontations ensued, resulting in the death of one coca grower and injuries to both growers and members of the security forces. After almost three weeks of tension, the Bolivian government signed a landmark agreement with coca growers permitting 3,200 hectares of coca to remain in the region for one year. Coca growers agreed to voluntarily eradicate approximately 3,000 hectares of coca by the end of the year to meet an 8,000-hectare eradication quota. The accord signed on October 3 represents a dramatic departure from the stilted efforts at dialogue that the U.S. government has impeded since the 1998 initiation of Plan Dignidad. Uncharacteristically, U.S. Embassy officials did not reject the accord outright. The agreement contains many potential pitfalls and areas for future misunderstanding, but the greater flexibility demonstrated by the Bolivian government, coca growers and the U.S. Embassy has provided a viable short-term solution to the present conflict and much-needed breathing space to seek more enduring proposals.

Despite the high social costs of the militarized forced eradication program, the price, purity and availability of cocaine entering the U.S. have remained steady. Increased coca production in Peru and Colombia has more than replaced quantities eradicated in Bolivia, demonstrating once again the validity of the balloon theory, which asserts that coca suppressed in one area expands into another in response to ongoing demand. Nonetheless, Bolivian governments face strong and ongoing U.S. pressure to continue the so-called "Bolivian success story." Yet, success is always measured in terms of coca eradicated and not by the well-being of the Bolivian people. Back in the Chapare, where coca leaves are openly sold even at anti-drug checkpoints, coca growers and soldiers alike catch their breath and await the inevitable renewal of conflict and violence.

The Emergence of "Supercoca"

Joshua Davis

Joshua Davis has been writing for *Wired* magazine since 2003. For this article on herbicide-resistant coca plants, called supercoca, Davis mixes serious, scientifically based analysis and interviews with genetic experts with descriptions of his own attempts to find and test samples of the coca plant in Colombia. Davis explains that coca plants have become increasingly resistant to U.S.-led coca-eradication efforts, either because drug lords have managed to genetically modify the plants and distribute resistant strains to coca farmers, or because coca farmers themselves have employed selective breeding to produce resistant plants that the farmers distribute to each other. In either scenario, the "supercoca" is a formidable obstacle to U.S. eradication programs.

I've got 23 ziplock bags filled with coca leaves laid out on the rickety table in front of me. It's been seven hours since the leaves were picked, and they're already secreting the raw alkaloid that gives cocaine its kick. The smell is pungently woody, but that may just be the mold growing on the walls of this dingy hotel room in the southern Colombian jungle. Somewhere down the hall, a woman is moaning with increasing urgency. I've barricaded the door in case the paramilitaries arrive.

I drop half a milliliter of water into a plastic test tube and mash a piece of a leaf inside. As the water tints green, I notice that my hands are shaking. I haven't slept for two days, and the Marxist guerrillas have this town encircled. But what's really making me nervous is the green liquid in the tube.

Over the past three years, rumors of a new strain of coca have circulated in the Colombian military. The new plant, samples of which are spread out on this table, goes by different names: supercoca, la millonaria. Here in the southern region it's known as Boliviana negra. The most impressive characteristic is not that it produces more leaves—though it does—but that it is resistant to glyphosate. The herbicide, known by its brand name, Roundup, is the key ingredient in the US-financed, billion-dollar aerial coca fumigation campaign that is a cornerstone of America's war on drugs.

The possible explanation: The farmers of the region may have used selective breeding to develop a hardier strain of coca. If a plant happened to demonstrate herbicide resistance, it would be more widely cultivated, and clippings would be either sold or, in many cases, given away or even stolen by other farmers. Such a peer-to-peer network could, over time, result in a coca crop that can withstand large-scale aerial spraying campaigns.

But experts in herbicide resistance suspect that there is another, more intriguing possibility: The coca plant may have been genetically modified in a lab. The technology is fairly trivial. In 1996, Monsanto commercialized its patented Roundup Ready soybean—a genetically modified plant impervious to glyphosate. The innovation ushered in an era of hyperefficient soybean production: Farmers were able to spray entire fields, killing all the weeds and leaving behind a thriving soybean crop. The arrival of Roundup Ready coca would have a similar effect—except that in this case, it would be the US doing the weed killing for the drug lords.

Whether its resistance came from selective breeding or genetic modification, the new strain poses a significant foreign-policy challenge to the US. How Washington responds depends on how the plant became glyphosate resistant. That's why I'm here in the jungle—to test for the new coca. I've brought along a mobile kit used to detect the presence of the Roundup Ready gene in soybean samples. If the tests are inconclusive, my backup plan is to smuggle the leaves to Colombia's capital, Bogotá, and have their DNA sequenced in a lab.

In my hotel room, I put the swizzle stick-sized test strip into the tube filled with mashed Boliviana negra. The green water snakes up the strip. If the midsection turns red, I'll know that the drug lords have genetically engineered the plant and beaten the US at its own game. If it doesn't, it'll mean that Colombia's farmers have outwitted 21st-century technology with an agricultural technique that's been around for 10,000 years.

Coca Crop Dusting

I first learned about the possibility of herbicide-resistant cocaine eight weeks before I arrived in South America. I was having a quiet Sunday brunch at home in California with a few friends and their Colombian guest. It was a beautiful day; we sat on the deck and chatted about upcoming vacation plans over waffles and grapefruit juice.

The conversation changed when the guest began talking about how he'd spent three years working in the military intelligence branch of the Colombian army, which has been waging a civil war against the guerrillas for four decades. His main assignment was to prevent insurgents from importing weapons and military technology.

After the US helped the Colombian military dismantle the Medellín and Cali cocaine cartels in the '90s, the guerrillas moved in and took over much of the drug trade. By the late '90s, rebels controlled more than a third of the country and had the financial clout to intensify the war and protect their newfound position as narcotraffickers. It's an extremely lucrative business. The coke habit in the US alone was worth $35 billion in 2000—about $10 billion more than Microsoft brought in that year.

But the most intriguing development he mentioned was regular reports of Roundup Ready coca. "We started to hear about this plant three years ago," he said. "We understood then that the spraying was not killing it, but nobody wants to talk about it because it might put an end to American aid money."

US aid to Colombia totaled more than $750 million [in 2003] and has been flooding in since 2000, when Congress approved the Clinton administration's Plan Colombia, a regional anti-narcotics package. About 20 percent of the money was devoted to maintaining a fleet of crop dusters and support planes that make almost daily sorties over the Colombia countryside. (The rest of the money went to economic support, military aid, and police training.) The crop dusters fly high, out of artillery range, until they reach a designated coca field, and then descend to spray the plants with a coating of Roundup. The concept is simple: Kill the coca and there will be no cocaine.

Explaining Modification

The day after our brunch, I looked up the Herbicide Resistance Action Committee and spoke with Ian Heap, the committee's chair. Heap is a global herbicide watchdog. If a farmer in Thailand notes that a certain weed is surviving repeated herbicide applications, local scientists will collect a sample and ship it to Corvallis, Oregon, where Heap runs a private laboratory. He is funded primarily by herbicide manufacturers who want to know how effective their products are. I figured he would know something about the reported resistance in coca. "So they've finally done it," he said with a breezy Australian accent. "I've been waiting for a call like this for a long time."

Heap explained that few people knew how to genetically manipulate plants until the early '90s. Then suddenly, even undergraduates were learning the techniques. At the same time, scientific papers were published that identified CP4, a gene responsible for glyphosate resistance. By the late '90s, it's easy to imagine the narcos hiring one unscrupulous scientist to tinker with coca. "Cocaine dealers have a lot of money to do the convincing," Heap said. "Genetically modifying the coca plant is the most obvious defense against fumigation. If I were a drug lord, it's what I would do."

Heap suspects that the US government might keep such a development quiet. The herbicide would still be effective against older, more widely planted coca strains, and, for a while at least, Colombia's eradication campaign would continue to show impressive results. But eventually, as the modified strain spread, coca cultivation would rise again, and spraying would have no effect. In the interim, farmers growing the new strain would get free weeding. "It's critical for the war on drugs that this gets independently checked out," Heap concluded. "But I'm sure as hell not going down there."

To get another view, I called Jonathan Gressel, one of the world's foremost experts on herbicide resistance and a professor of plant science at the Weizmann Institute of Science in Israel. "The only surprise is that the drug mafia didn't do it sooner," Gressel said when I told him about reports of glyphosate-resistant coca. "Privately, my colleagues and I have been predicting this for years."

Another way to explain the reported resistance, he said, was that over time the plants developed it naturally after repeated exposure. But in the case of coca, he estimated that it would take 20 years of constant spraying before a naturally resistant strain of the plant would establish itself. It was possible that farmers beat the odds and got lucky in the four years of intensive spraying. "But the most reasonable explanation," Gressel told me, "is that the illicit narcotics world has genetically engineered the coca plant to be resistant to glyphosate."

The only way to know for sure was to find the plant and test it. . . .

The Beginnings of Super Coca

Don Miguel [the author's guide] tells me that Boliviana negra appeared in the region three years ago and is now spreading rapidly across the countryside—just as the herbicide experts told me it might. The new strain is disseminated via cuttings; farmers cut off stems and sell them. Some farmers, looking to make more money, travel with their cuttings and peddle them around the region. And once a farmer grows a new plant, he can sell his own cuttings. It's file-swapping brought to the jungle—a highly efficient decentralized distribution chain.

Don Miguel doesn't know where the strain originated. He has heard rumors of a group of mysterious agronomists who develop better coca plants for the traffickers, but he doesn't know where they are or anything about them.

He does have a clear sense of how the new plant is affecting his region. At first, he says, the aerial spraying was successful, but now, with the arrival of Boliviana negra, it's affecting only those who are growing lawful crops. "The truth is that the fumigation drives us to the one thing that will survive—and that is Boliviana negra," he says. "Not bananas, not yucca, not maize."

The Colombian and US governments want farmers to grow legal crops, he explains, and in the past have paid them to eradicate coca. But though American embassy officials insist that the spraying campaign is more than 99 percent accurate, Don Miguel says that almost all the farmers he knows and represents report that legal crops are sprayed as well. He says that his own tree farm was sprayed, pushing him to the edge of bankruptcy. If Boliviana negra will guarantee income for farmers, Don Miguel says, they will grow it and have less incentive to discuss eradication with the government.

Not to mention the financial benefits. One hectare of land in Putumayo will produce $100 of corn. The same plot will produce $1,000 of coca. Plus you don't have to transport the coca—the guerrillas will come to your farm and collect it. So why would anyone grow corn? "Because if you grow coca," Don Miguel says, "you deal with the guerrillas or the paramilitaries or both, and they kill whenever they want."

Don Miguel has another fear. He doesn't believe that the US

will tolerate the existence of glyphosate-resistant coca. When the authorities find out that farmers are growing the new coca, he fears it will be only a matter of time before they switch to a new herbicide.

Switching to Fusarium

He has reason for concern. Last summer [2004], documents show, anti-narcotics officials at the US embassy in Bogotá quietly approached Colombia's president, Álvaro Uribe, and asked him if he'd consider switching from Roundup to *Fusarium oxysporum*, a plant-killing fungus classified as a mycoherbicide. Some species are known to attack coca; in the early '90s, a natural Fusarium outbreak decimated the Peruvian coca crop.

But Fusarium is not a chemical—it's a fungus, and it can live on in the soil. A proposal to consider using it in Florida in 1999 was rejected after the head of the state's Department of Environmental Protection found that it was "difficult, if not impossible, to control [Fusarium's] spread" and that the "mutated fungi can cause disease in a large number of crops, including tomatoes, peppers, flowers, corn, and vines." A switch to Fusarium would, at the least, be an escalation in the herbicide war and a tacit acknowledgment of glyphosate's failure. It could also turn out to be the A-bomb of herbicides.

Still, according to a letter sent from the State Department to Colombia's US ambassador, Uribe was "ready to learn more." The letter, dated October 3, 2003, laid out steps for moving this plan forward, but when I spoke to officials at the embassy, they vehemently denied they are considering a herbicide switch. They stated that they are thrilled with the success of Roundup.

Don Miguel admits that on one level, the spraying has been highly effective. Almost all the old strains of coca have been eradicated. What's left are small plots of Boliviana negra, but these have become more productive, in part because the spraying has killed all the other plants competing for nutrients.

US Denial

US officials point to the eradication results of the past three years and argue that the plant could not possibly be resistant. A high-ranking US anti-narcotics official who declined to be identified told me that she had never heard of Boliviana negra, la millonaria, or any Roundup Ready coca plant. Another American official began our conversation by saying, "So you're here to talk about the nonexistent glyphosate-resistant coca?" And then, more forcefully, "These campesinos have zero education. They can't be trusted to know whether a plant is resistant to glyphosate." Nonetheless, I was assured that a helicopter would be dispatched to Putumayo to search for samples. Even amid increasing reports of resistant superstrains, officials have yet to find any evidence of them.

Perhaps they haven't been to La Hormiga. Everyone I talk to here knows about the resistant plant. Three hours after leaving the coca fields, I attend a meeting of two dozen heads of local farmer cooperatives—they represent more than 5,000 farmers in Putumayo—and they nod knowingly when asked about the new breed. "Nobody listens to us because they think we are dumb farmers," says one man. "The Americans are arrogant. They don't talk to the people who live here. We are the ones who are sprayed. We are the ones who live with the plants.". . .

Conclusion: Selective Breeding

Four weeks later, the scientist [the author has employed] sends me an email saying that he has completed the DNA analysis and found no evidence of modification. He tested specifically for the presence of CP4—a telltale indicator of the Roundup Ready modification—as well as for the cauliflower mosaic virus, the gene most commonly used to insert foreign DNA into a plant. It is still possible that the plant has been genetically modified using other genes, but not likely. Discovering new methods of engineering glyphosate resistance would require the best scientific minds and years of organized research. And given that there is already a published methodology, there would be little reason to duplicate the effort.

Which points back to selective breeding. The implication is that the farmers' decentralized system of disseminating coca cuttings has been amazingly effective—more so than genetic engineering could hope to be. When one plant somewhere in the country demonstrated tolerance to glyphosate, cuttings were made and passed on to dealers and farmers, who could sell them quickly to farmers hoping to withstand the spraying. The best of the next generation was once again used for cuttings and distributed.

This technique—applied over four years—is now the most likely explanation for the arrival of Boliviana negra. By spraying so much territory, the US significantly increased the odds of generating beneficial mutations. There are numerous species of coca, further increasing the diversity of possible mutations. And in the Amazonian region, nature is particularly adaptive and resilient.

"I thought it was unlikely," says Gressel, the plant scientist at the Weizmann Institute. "But farmers aren't dumb. They obviously spotted a lucky mutation and propagated the hell out of it."

The effects of this are far-reaching for American policymakers: A new herbicide would work only for a limited time against such a simple but effective ad hoc network. The coca-growing community is clearly primed to take advantage of any mutations.

A genetic laboratory is not as nimble. A lab is limited by research that is publicly available. In the case of Fusarium, the coca-killing fungus and likely successor to glyphosate, there is no body of work discussing genetically induced resistance. If the government switched to Fusarium, a scientist would have to perform ground-breaking genetic research to fashion a Fusarium-resistant coca plant.

The reality is that a smoothly functioning selective-breeding system is a greater threat to US antidrug efforts. Certainly government agents can switch to Fusarium and enjoy some short-term results. But after a few years—during which legal crops could be devastated—a new strain of Fusarium-resistant coca would likely emerge, one just as robust as the glyphosate-resistant strain.

The drug war in Colombia presupposes that it's eventually possible to destroy cocaine at its source. But the facts on the ground suggest this is no longer possible. In this war, it's hard to beat technology developed 10,000 years ago.

Crack in the Twenty-First Century

Geoffrey Gray

Geoffrey Gray is a freelance writer living in Manhattan who publishes regularly in New York magazines and weeklies. In this article for a local news weekly, Gray analyzes the state of crack in 2004. Rather than smoking the drug these days, some users prefer to inject it, he writes. Nonetheless, Gray's conclusion is that crack is on the way out as the drug of choice. Through a comparison of the crack "epidemic" of the 1980s and the crack world now, Gray concludes that there are few new users of the drug, despite little price change. He also maintains that harsh prison sentences for dealing and possession have contributed to crack's decline, as other drugs take its place.

When he first began to go get it, Louie Jones found himself in abandoned Harlem buildings, places crowded with shattered glass, broken mirrors, newfound junkies and prostitutes all "geeking and tweaking." They were places where one pull could cost $1 and be lit from an anonymous worker behind a wall; where pipes or stems and torches could be rented for $3 a night; where one small rock of crack cocaine, then the new jewel of the ghetto, could cost as little as $5.

Altogether, 10 minutes of intense, pounding euphoria—a little more, depending on the quality of the crack—could cost about the same price as a Happy Meal at McDonald's. Sellers would bark their jingles onto the street like circus carnies.

Geoffrey Gray, "On the Rocks," *City Limits, New York's Urban Affairs Newsmagazine,* March 2004. Copyright © 2004 by City Limits Community Information Services, Inc. Reproduced by permission.

"Jumbo crack. Jumbo crack. Rock so big gonna make you come back!"

The price of crack hasn't changed much over the years, and neither has its attraction to users looking for a drug bargain. But virtually everything about the crack experience—including its delivery, its use, its availability and its profitability—is profoundly different.

For one thing, many users don't smoke crack anymore. They shoot it. Users heat up the rock, mix it with lemon juice or vinegar or rubbing alcohol—"soup," it's sometimes called—and inject the serum. This technique first appeared as early as the mid-1980s and has grown steadily in popularity.

"Injecting crack is a phenomenon happening all across the country," says Stephen Lankenau, an ethnographer who tracked users in 10 American cities for a National Institute for Drug Abuse study that concluded two years ago. Lankenau says that liquid crack has become a cheap substitute for powder cocaine. The effect is a more prolonged high, sometimes over an hour, instead of the 10- to 15-minute rush that comes from sucking on a crack pipe. Shooting up also eliminates the frequent pangs—"geeking and tweaking"—and allows users "to just chill," as Jones puts it. There's a downside, of course: Injecting any drug through needles poses the threat of HIV, hepatitis and other health disasters.

Crack Not as Profitable

The business of crack is also a very different game today. Jones, a former user and dealer who now works as a drug-awareness advisor with the Harm Reduction Coalition and other groups supporting users' rights, says he remembers dealers raking in as much as $1,500 to $2,500 an hour selling crack in the mid-1980s and early 1990s—often more during the first four days of the month. Those are a dealer's best days because that's when most government-issued assistance checks arrive in the mail. With high demand, dealers could unload the drugs quickly. Bundles of a hundred plastic vials filled with crack, "100 packs," could disappear in hours.

During the boom, check cashing places and barren spots in East New York, Brownsville, parts of Harlem, Washington Heights, and other neighborhoods were havens for dealers, as well as for prostitutes looking to sell themselves for drug money. There were "crackheads," then "crack whores," then "crack babies." Whole blocks were caught in turf wars as dealers battled over their market shares, fueling a rise in violent shootouts. Crack was an epidemic, and the mixture of baking soda and cocaine became part of the city's cultural fabric.

Today, dealers are lucky to pull in $1,500 a week in sales, says Jones. Law enforcement is stricter than for other drugs, and there are other, less-stigmatized substances to choose from, like methamphetamines, powder cocaine and the ever-popular marijuana. The abandoned buildings and street corners where crack was once purchased are increasingly being replaced by a more flexible network of dealers, Jones says. Operators use cars to deliver crack, along with other drugs, or deal from apartment buildings. A lot of dealers don't even carry crack anymore. "Then, the game was 24-7," says Jones. "Now, it's like 9-5."

One reason business is so slow is that there are virtually no new crack users—only the same users getting older. "Crack has followed the classic epidemic pattern," says Andrew Golub, principal investigator at the National Development and Research Institute. He's been tracking trends among drug users for the last 12 years, since crack first started to slip. "The infected period," he says, "is through." The typical crack user, Golub says, is a longtime consumer, male, age 30 to 45, and lives on a fixed income.

Still Lingering

No longer a main dish for drug users, crack is often now a nostalgic accompaniment to other drugs like speed and marijuana. It's also being used as a cheap supplement to counter the effects of other drugs. "The new crack users are heroin users," says Julia Delancey, a single room occupancy hotel supervisor at Citywide Harm Reduction. A former addict who works daily with drug users in city-sponsored homeless hotels, Delancey says that many of her clients have been using crack to "balance themselves out"—as a means to mitigate the post-high strain of heroin.

Crack's packaging has also changed. Mostly gone are the plastic vials, with different-colored lids differentiating quality or turf. Today, crack is typically purchased in small, pinkie-finger-sized plastic baggies—harder to identify and easier to hide in orifices.

Still Cheap, Still Dangerous

But what hasn't changed is the price: Two small pinkie bags can come as cheap as $5. That's hardly a big mark-up—and a lot of legal risk for little profit. Notes one Harlem confidant who's friendly with dealers: "[dealers] can make more money bootlegging cigarettes on the street now than selling crack—and you don't have to do any time."

Between the diminishing profits, threat of long jail sentences and a shrinking market, crack's future is dim. "Without a new make-up, a new presentation, new delivery and a new look, crack will be off the map," says Jones.

But this is New York, after all, and you can cop crack on the street—it's just tougher to find. And when you do find it, it might not be called crack. According to federal investigators at the Office of National Drug Control Policy, an agency that monitors drug use across the United States, nicknames now in use across the country include yums, cookies, girl, lady, loose, piedra, scottie, shrile, monkey nut (i.e., a big piece), pebbles, bird, rock star and twinkie.

And, just as it evolved in Darwinian fashion, crack might not become extinct so much as mutate. It might be injected more. It might appear faintly, laced against marijuana in blunts called "woolies" or wedged on the tip of cigarettes called "coolies." It might be cut into crystal meth or in a combo with PCP called "space base." It might be found wherever cheap elixirs can bring quick thrills and take the pain away.

"The desire doesn't change much, and the condition of people using hasn't changed much," says Jones. "Just the packaging and delivery."

How Drugs Are Classified

The Controlled Substances Act of 1970 classified drugs into five different lists, or schedules, in order of decreasing potential for abuse. The decision to place a drug on a particular schedule is based mainly on the effects the drug has on the body, mind, and behavior. However, other factors are also considered. The schedule is used to help establish the penalties for someone using or selling illegal drugs. On the other hand, sometimes a potentially valuable drug for treating a disease can be incorrectly scheduled, greatly hampering the exploration of its usefulness as a treatment.

Schedule of Controlled Substances

RATING	EXAMPLE
SCHEDULE I A high potential for abuse; no currently accepted medical use in the United States; or no accepted safety for use in treatment under medical supervision.	• Heroin • LSD • Marijuana • Mescaline • MDMA (Ecstasy) • PCP
SCHEDULE II A high potential for abuse; currently accepted medical use with severe restrictions; abuse of the substance may lead to severe psychological or physical dependence.	• Opium and Opiates • Demerol • Codeine • Percodan • Methamphetamines • Cocaine • Amphetamines
SCHEDULE III A potential for abuse less than the substances listed in Schedules I and II; currently accepted medical use in the United States; abuse may lead to moderate or low physical dependence or high psychological dependence.	• Anabolic steroids • Hydrocodone • Certain barbiturates • Hallucinogenic substances

Schedule of Controlled Substances

RATING	EXAMPLE
SCHEDULE IV A low potential for abuse relative to the substances listed in Schedule III; currently accepted medical use in the United States; limited physical or psychological dependence relative to the substances listed in Schedule III.	• Barbiturates • Narcotics • Stimulants
SCHEDULE V A low potential for abuse relative to the substances listed in Schedule III; currently accepted medical use in the United States; limited physical or psychological dependence relative to the substances listed in Schedule IV.	• Compounds with limited codeine such as cough medicine

Facts About Cocaine

Cocaine is an extract of *Erythroxylon coca*, the coca plant.

The coca plant is native to the Andean mountain region, where it thrives at high altitudes.

Seventy-five percent of the world's coca grown for processing into cocaine is found in Colombia.

Cocaine's most common form is a whitish powder. Cocaine can also take the form of a liquid or a paste.

Cocaine in powdered form can be snorted up the nose, where it is absorbed in the nasal passages. In liquid form it can be injected with a hypodermic syringe, and in paste form it can be rubbed into the mucous membranes. It can also be dissolved in a beverage and drunk.

Chewing the dried leaves of the coca plant produces a milder version of the effects of powdered cocaine.

Crack is a form of cocaine that has been processed with baking soda and liquid and heated to take on a solid, smokable form.

Crack cocaine usually comes in the form of "rocks," which look like small, whitish or brown pieces of gravel.

Cocaine is a stimulant, as opposed to a depressant, that affects the central nervous system.

The physical effects of cocaine include hyperactivity, increased blood pressure, and increased temperature.

The psychological effects of cocaine include a sense of euphoria, mental clarity, reduced fatigue, a feeling of reduced need for food and water, and feelings of irritability, restlessness, and anxiety.

The effects of cocaine can last anywhere from a few minutes to several hours, depending on the form of the drug and how it was ingested.

Regular cocaine users are at risk of malnourishment due to the drug's tendency to reduce a user's desire for food.

Cocaine is frequently cut with various fillers by dealers in an attempt to increase their profits. Common fillers include baby powder, evaporated milk, and the local anesthetic lidocaine.

An overdose of cocaine can cause heart attack, seizures, respiratory failure, and stroke.

Cocaine-related deaths are usually caused by a heart attack followed by respiratory failure.

Cocaine is classified by the Food and Drug Administration as a Schedule II drug, meaning it is at high risk of being abused but is accepted for medical treatment in the United States.

Possessors and dealers of crack cocaine receive longer federal sentences than those received by users or sellers of any other drug.

Cocaine addiction can be treated with pharmacological drugs or behavioral treatments, such as drug rehabilitation programs.

1500 B.C.
The ancient Incans first domesticate and begin raising the coca plant.

A.D. 1577
Nicolas Mondares, a Spanish priest and doctor living in Peru, records the first known description of the coca bush. Coca is imported to Europe.

1859
The first shipment of coca leaves is ordered and received by Friedrich Wohler, a well-known German scientist.

1860
Cocaine is distilled from the coca plant by Alfred Niemann, a German graduate student working in Friedrich Wohler's laboratory.

1863
Chemist Angelo Mariani creates the first commercial cocaine tonic, "Vin Mariani," with coca extract dissolved in wine. The drink was touted as a healthful tonic, suitable for treating a variety of ills.

1884
Viennese physician Karl Koller discovers that cocaine is an effective anesthetic for eye surgery. Sigmund Freud publishes *Uber Coca*, his seminal article on the beneficial effects of cocaine, establishing cocaine's popularity among the medical community. Cocaine becomes available to the general public.

1886
Coca-Cola, containing cocaine, is invented by pharmacist J.S. Pemberton in Atlanta, Georgia, as a nonalcoholic alternative to coca wine.

1887
Cocaine is declared the official remedy of the United States Hay Fever Association.

1906
The Pure Food and Drug Act is passed by Congress, requiring that cocaine, among other substances, be labeled as an ingredient on product packaging.

1909
The United States begins controlling the international traffic of habit-forming drugs by holding the International Opium Commission in Shanghai.

1914
The Harrison Narcotic Act is passed by Congress, prohibiting use of cocaine without a physician's prescription. The *New York Times* prints "Negro Cocaine 'Fiends' New Southern Menace" by Dr. Edward Huntington Williams, setting off a wave of racially motivated fears about the effects of the drug on the African American community in the South.

1922
Cocaine is officially declared an illegal narcotic.

1969
Music producer Phil Spector buys cocaine from actors Dennis Hopper and Peter Fonda in the movie *Easy Rider*, marking the first time cocaine is shown in a modern film. Cocaine's influence in popular culture begins to rise.

1980
"Freebasing" becomes known to the mainstream world through the media when comedian Richard Pryor sets himself on fire while converting cocaine to freebase, the predecessor to crack cocaine.

1982
Cocaine use among eighteen- to twenty-five-year-olds rises to an all-time high, with 28 percent reporting that they had tried the drug. Cocaine Anonymous is founded in Los Angeles.

1985
Somewhere in Los Angeles, crack is distilled from powdered cocaine and rapidly gains popularity. Dr. Ira Chasnoff publishes his landmark article in *New England Journal of Medicine* about the effects of prenatal cocaine exposure on infants. The term *crack baby* is coined in the media.

1986
President Ronald Reagan officially declares that the United States has begun a "war on drugs." The Anti–Drug Abuse Act is passed, setting different sentence limits for possessors of powdered cocaine versus

possessors of crack cocaine. Media coverage of crack cocaine hits an all-time high.

1989

President George H.W. Bush makes crack and cocaine the center of his national address on federal drug control strategy. The nation's first drug czar, William Bennett, is appointed. Bush begins the Andean Initiative, which provides U.S. military and economic aid to Bolivia for reducing coca-farming.

1993

Pablo Escobar, the leader of one of Latin America's largest drug cartels that controlled much of the flow of cocaine into the United States, is killed by Colombian security forces in a targeted attack.

1997

Under pressure from the United States, Bolivia initiates its Plan Dignidad, its first nationwide plan to eradicate illegal coca in the country.

2000

The United States launches Plan Colombia, a $1.6 billion aid package to the country, designed to eradicate coca-growing and, thus, reduce the flow of cocaine into the United States.

2004

Concerns arise about the possible existence of genetically modified, herbicide-resistant coca. Eradication programs continue with increased funding from the United States and Latin American governments.

ORGANIZATIONS TO CONTACT

The editors have compiled the following list of organizations concerned with the issues debated in this book. The descriptions are derived from materials provided by the organizations. All have publications or information available for interested readers. The list was compiled on the date of publication of the present volume; the information provided here may change. Be aware that many organizations take several weeks or longer to respond to inquiries, so allow as much time as possible.

American Academy of Addiction Psychiatry (AAAP)

1010 Vermont Ave. NW, Suite 710, Washington, DC 20005
(202) 393-4484 • fax: (202) 393-4419
Web site: www.aaap.org

The AAAP is a scientific and professional organization formed to provide support and continuing education for addiction and mental health specialists. It provides research money and opportunities for its members as well as holding professional conferences. The AAAP publishes *The American Journal on Addiction* and a newsletter, *The AAAP News.*

American Council on Drug Education (ACDE)

164 W. Seventy-fourth St., New York, NY 10023
(800) 488-DRUG
e-mail: acde@phoenixhouse.org • Web site: www.acde.org

The ACDE is a private agency that creates programs and accompanying materials for drug abuse education. The organization states that it uses the latest scientific research in the field to provide educators and employers with aids for their substance abuse programs. The ACDE publishes numerous pamphlets, lesson plans, and videos.

American Society of Addiction Medicine (ASAM)

4601 North Park Ave., Arcade Suite 101, Chevy Chase, MD 20815
(301) 656-3920 • fax: (301) 656-3815
e-mail: email@asam.org • Web site: www.asam.org

The ASAM is a professional organization for physicians and other healthcare professionals who specialize in the study and treatment of drug addiction. The group disseminates information about the latest advances in drug addiction treatment and educates the public about drug treatment options. ASAM publishes *Journal of Addictive Diseases* and *ASAM News.*

Cocaine Anonymous (CA)

3740 Overland Ave., Suite C, Los Angeles, CA 90034
(310) 559-5833
e-mail: cawso@ca.org • Web site: www.ca.org

Cocaine Anonymous is a twelve-step program for cocaine addicts who wish to stop using the drug. The organization, structured similarly to Alcoholics Anonymous, consists of group meetings throughout the country where addicts can share their experiences in an anonymous environment. CA publishes a variety of pamphlets outlining the twelve-step program.

Drug Policy Alliance

925 Fifteenth St., 2nd Fl., Washington, DC 20005
(202) 216-0035 • fax: (202) 216-0803
e-mail: dc@drugpolicy.org • Web site: www.dpf.org

The Drug Policy Alliance works to end the "war on drugs" by encouraging public debate about drug policy and promoting alternatives to current drug control strategy through lobbying and public education. The group promotes the legalization and regulation of drugs, including cocaine. The alliance publishes a quarterly newsletter and other materials aimed at promoting treatment instead of incarceration for drug addicts.

Drug Prevention Network of the Americas (DPNA)

(979) 575-8516
e-mail: stephanie_hayes@bbtco.com • Web site: www.dpna.org

The DPNA is a nonprofit group that works to prevent drug abuse in the Western Hemisphere. This coalition of nongovernmental organizations from North and South America promotes a drug-free lifestyle and opposes the legalization of drugs. The DPNA publishes a monthly newsletter as well as a variety of documents, in Spanish and English, gathered from its various member groups.

Drug Reform Coordination Network (DRCnet)

1623 Connecticut Ave. NW, 3rd Fl., Washington, DC 20009
(202) 293-8340 • fax: (202) 293-8344
e-mail: drcnet@drcnet.org • Web site: www.stopthedrugwar.org

DRCnet is a drug policy reform organization that opposes the current national drug policy. The nonprofit group supports legalization of various drugs, including cocaine, opposes mandatory sentencing laws for nonviolent drug offenders, and works for patients' right to use currently illegal drugs for medical reasons. DRCnet maintains the online Schaffer Library of Drug Policy.

Drug Strategies

1755 Massachusetts Ave. NW, Suite 821, Washington, DC 20036
(202) 289-9070
e-mail: dspolicy@aol.com • Web site: www.drugstrategies.org

Drug Strategies is a nonprofit organization that monitors the nation's drug control policy annually and provides funds on a state and local level to aid drug prevention efforts. The group produces studies of drug abuse programs and reviews drug education programs in schools. Drug Strategies publishes many annual reports, including *Keeping Score*, a yearly review of federal drug control spending.

Narconon International
7060 Hollywood Blvd, Suite 220, Hollywood, CA 90028
(323) 962-2404 • fax: (323) 962-6872
e-mail: rehab@narconon.org • Web site: www.narconon.org

This national nonprofit organization offers drug rehabilitation programs throughout the country. Narconon runs rehab centers for addicts as well as drug education and drug prevention programs, all focusing specifically on abuse of narcotics, legal and illegal. The organization publishes its *First Step Program Series*, which takes the reader through the Narconon process, as well as other books and pamphlets for addicts wanting to quit and their families.

National Center on Addiction and Substance Abuse (CASA)
633 Third Avenue, 19th Fl., New York, NY 10017
(212) 841-5200
Web site: www.casacolumbia.org

CASA, which is run out of Columbia University, functions as a think tank for drug abuse issues. CASA holds conferences and produces articles in an effort to educate the public about the costs, economic and social, of drug abuse; to encourage others to fight drug addiction; to support those who are already researching drug abuse; and to assess treatment programs and law enforcement techniques. The center's publications include staff reports on various drug issues and a quarterly newsletter, *CASA Inside*.

National Institute on Drug Abuse (NIDA)
6001 Executive Blvd., Room 5213, Bethesda, MD 20892
(301) 443-1124
e-mail: information@lists.nida.nih.gov
Web site: www.drugabuse.gov

NIDA is a section of the National Institutes of Health, which is a subsidiary of the federal Department of Health and Human Services. The institute, funded by the federal government, focuses on applying scientific advances to decrease drug abuse and addiction, and it supports most of the world's research on drug abuse. NIDA publishes research monographs, as well as books on specific drugs, treatments, and science education programs related to drug abuse.

Office of National Drug Control Policy (ONDCP)
750 Seventeenth St., Washington, DC 20503
(800) 666-3332 • fax: (301) 519-5212
e-mail: ondcp@ncjrs.org
Web site: www.whitehousedrugpolicy.gov

ONDCP establishes the goals and objectives for the White House's drug control programs. It works to reduce illegal drug use and trafficking, to end drug-related crime, and to spread awareness of drug-related health effects. The office works closely with the national Drug Enforcement Agency (DEA) and publishes numerous documents on various aspects of illegal drugs, including drug fact sheets, the president's *National Drug Control Strategy*, and various public service pamphlets.

Partnership for a Drug-Free America
405 Lexington Ave., Suite 1601, New York, NY 10174
(212) 922-1560 • fax: (212) 922-1570
Web site: www.drugfreeamerica.org

The partnership is a nonprofit organization that utilizes media communication to reduce demand for illicit drugs in America. Best known for its national antidrug advertising campaign, the partnership works to "unsell" drugs to children and to prevent drug use among kids. It publishes the annual *Partnership Newsletter* as well as monthly press releases about current events with which the partnership is involved.

Washington Office on Latin America (WOLA)
1630 Connecticut Ave. NW, Suite 200, Washington, DC 20009
(202) 797-2171 • fax: (202) 797-2172
e-mail: wola@wola.org • Web site: www.wola.org

WOLA is a nongovernmental organization (NGO) that focuses its efforts on human rights and peace work in Latin America. WOLA provides information and analysis to Congress, other NGOs, and the international media. The group publishes a newsletter, *CrossCurrents*, and many reports monitoring the drug situation in Bolivia, Colombia, and Peru.

FOR FURTHER RESEARCH

Books

Richard Ashley, *Cocaine: Its History, Uses, and Effects*. New York: Warner, 1976.

Belén Boville, *The Cocaine War*. New York: Algora, 2004.

Patrick L. Clawson, *The Andean Cocaine Industry*. New York: St. Martin's, 1996.

David Courtwright, *Dark Paradise: Opiate Addiction in America Before 1940*. Cambridge, MA: Harvard University Press, 1982.

John C. Flynn, *Cocaine: An In-Depth Look at the Facts, Science, History, and Future of the World's Most Addictive Drug*. Secaucus, NJ: Carol Publishing Group, 1991.

Stephen Hyde, ed., *Writers on Cocaine*. New York: Thunder's Mouth, 2002.

Steven B. Karch, *A Brief History of Cocaine*. Boca Raton, FL: CRC, 1998.

———, *A History of Cocaine: The Mystery of Coca Java and the Kew Plant*. London: Royal Society of Medicine, 2003.

Joseph Kennedy, *Coca Exotica: The Illustrated Story of Cocaine*. New York: Cornwall, 1985.

Rensselaer W. Lee III, *The White Labryinth: Cocaine and Political Power*. New Brunswick, NJ: Transaction, 1991.

Edmundo Morales, *Cocaine: White Gold Rush in Peru*. Tucson: University of Arizona Press, 1989.

David F. Musto, *The American Disease: Origins of Narcotic Control*. New Haven, CT: Yale University Press, 1987.

Mark Pendergrast, *For God, Country, and Coca-Cola: The Unauthorized History of the Great American Soft Drink and the Company*. New York: Scribner's, 1993.

Joel Phillips, *Cocaine: The Mystique and the Reality*. New York: Avon, 1980.

Jerome J. Platt, *Cocaine Addiction: Theory, Research, and Treatment*. Cambridge, MA: Harvard University Press, 1997.

Jimmie L. Reeves, *Cracked Coverage: Television News, the Anti-Cocaine*

Crusade, and the Reagan Legacy. Durham, NC: Duke University Press, 1994.

Craig Reinarman and Harry Levine, eds., *Crack in America: Demon Drugs and Social Justice.* Berkeley: University of California Press, 1997.

Kevin Riley, *Snow Job? The War Against International Cocaine Trafficking.* New Brunswick, NJ: Transaction, 1996.

Claire E. Sterk, *Fast Lives: Women Who Use Crack Cocaine.* Philadelphia: Temple University Press, 1999.

Dominic Streatfeild, *Cocaine: An Unauthorized Biography.* New York: St. Martin's, 1998.

Gary Webb, *Dark Alliance: The CIA, the Contras, and the Crack Cocaine Explosion.* New York: Seven Stories, 1999.

Andrew T. Weil, *The Natural Mind.* Boston: Houghton Mifflin, 1986.

Terry Williams, *Crackhouse: Notes from the End of the Line.* New York: Addison Wesley, 1992.

Periodicals

Sharon Begley, "Hope for 'Snow Babies,'" *Newsweek*, September 29, 1997.

Peter Canby, "Latin America's Longest War," *Nation*, August 16, 2004.

Ira Chasnoff, "Cocaine Use in Pregnancy," *New England Journal of Medicine*, 1985.

Congressional Digest, "Colombian Drug Threat," February 2001.

———, "Minimum Sentencing and Cocaine Use," January 2003.

David T. Courtwright, "The Hidden Epidemic: Opiate Addiction and Cocaine Use in the South, 1860–1920," *Journal of Southern History*, February 1983.

Tony Dajer, "Snowed," *Discover*, October 1998.

Steven Dudley, "On the Road with the FARC," *Progressive*, November 2003.

Ecologist, "Cocaine Colonialism," October 1999.

Economist, "The Andean Coca Wars," March 4, 2000.

———, "Coca Clashes," August 17, 1996.

———, "Coca's Second Front," January 6, 2001.

———, "The Price of Powder," November 11, 2004.

———, "Trouble for Plan Colombia," August 4, 2001.

———, "The Weedkiller War," September 7, 2003.

Jan Farrington, "Resisting Cocaine's Tragic Lure," *Current Health*, February 1999.

J.J. Forno, "Cocaine Abuse: The Evolution from Coca Leaves to Freebase," *Journal of Drug Education*, 1981.

Katharine Greider, "Crackpot Ideas," *Mother Jones*, July/August 1995.

Harper's Magazine, "Blow, Winds, and Crack Your Cheeks," May 2004.

Harvard Mental Health Letter, "The Crack Baby Myth," September 2001.

David Hatchett, "Crackin' Down on Crack and Crime," *Crisis*, October 1995.

Dorothy K. Hatsukami, "Is Crack 100 Times 'Worse' than Cocaine?" *DATA: The Brown University Digest of Addiction Theory & Application*, April 1997.

Jo Ann Kawell, "Coke & the CIA: The Real Thing?" *Nation*, September 28, 1998.

Randall Kennedy, "Is Everything Race?" *New Republic*, January 1, 1996.

J.B. Mattison, "Cocaine Dosage and Cocaine Addiction," *Lancet*, May 21, 1887.

Tim McGirk, "A Carpet of Cocaine," *Time*, August 9, 1999.

Judy Monroe, "Cocaine a Killer," *Current Health*, March 1997.

Tom Morganthau, "Kids and Cocaine," *Newsweek*, March 1986.

David F. Musto, "International Traffic in Coca Through the Early 20th Century," *Drug and Alcohol Dependence*, 1998.

———, "Opium, Cocaine, and Marijuana in American History," *Scientific American*, July 1991.

———, "Perception and Regulation of Drug Use: The Rise and Fall of the Tide," *Annals of Internal Medicine*, September 15, 1996.

————, "Why Did Sherlock Holmes Use Cocaine?" *Baker Street Journal*, December 1998.

Tim Padgett, "Coke Floats," *Time*, December 11, 2001.

Linda Robinson, "The Cocaine Connection," *U.S. News & World Report*, May 29, 2000.

Tina Rosenberg, "The Great Cocaine Quagmire," *Rolling Stone*, April 12, 2001.

Jill Smolowe, "One Drug, Two Sentences," *Time*, June 19, 1995.

Monique Stauder, "Columbia's Cocaine Frontier," *Mother Jones*, November/December 2001.

Time, "Powder Blues," October 29, 2001.

Carlos Villalon, "Cocaine Country," *National Geographic*, July 2004.

Gregory L. Vistica, "Was the CIA Involved in the Crack Epidemic?" *Newsweek*, September 30, 1996.

Andrew Weil, "The New Politics of Coca," *New Yorker*, May 15, 1995.

Kate Wheeler, "Coca Fiend," *Outside*, October 2004.

Coletta Youngers, "Cocaine Madness," *NACLA Report on the Americas*, November/December 2000.

INDEX

addiction, 37–40
  danger of, 130
  denial of, 48
  methods to combat, 17
  personal account of, 49–55
Adler, Patricia, 98, 99
African Americans
  crack and, 16
  drug economy and, 102–104,
    120–26
  sentencing laws and, 116–19
  see also inner cities
Aigner, Thomas G., 69
animal studies, 68–69
Anslinger, Harry J., 59, 60, 61
antidrug advertising, 92
antidrug education, 92–93

Balster, Robert L., 69
bankers, drug, 99–102
Bánzer, Hugo, 134
Barco, Virgilio, 90
basuco, 106
Beer, Peter, 102
Bennett, Bill, 88, 97
Bentley, W.H., 33
Bias, Len, 118
Biden, Joseph, 118
blacks. See African Americans
Blau, Charles, 101
Bolivia
  cultivation of coca in, 16–17,
    73–74
  U.S. efforts to stop coca
    production in, 132–40
Bolivian negra. See supercoca
Bourgois, Philippe, 120
Bourne, Peter, 64–65
Boys, Annabel, 128–29
Brücke, Ernst, 40
bugs, 65–66
Bush, George H.W., 16, 86
  drug control strategy of, 86–97
  money laundering and, 101

California, money laundering in,
    101–102
Candler, Asa G., 57
Capital Bank, 100, 102
Catholic Church, 21–22
Chiles, Lawton, 118
Cieza de León, Pedro, 21
Coca-Cola, 14, 56–62
coca culture, in South America,
    20–25, 73–75
  see also coca plant
cocaine, 13
  adulterated, 80
  coca vs., 76
  dangers of, 129–31
  demand for, 77, 98–99
  discovery of, 14–15
  effects of, 13, 65–68, 73
  Freud's experiences with, 32–40
  future of, 17–18
  imports, 58–60
  increases in use of, 128–29
  injection of, 47
  in popular culture, 15
  popularity of, 68–69, 72–73
  psychosis, 67–68
  public tolerance of, 64–65
  regulation of, 15
  research on, 65–68
  self-experiments with, 42–47
  as status symbol, 79–85
  whores, 114–15
  see also crack; drug control
    policies; drug economy
Cocaine Kids (Williams), 103
coca plant, 13–14
  cultivation of, 73–74
  distillation of cocaine from, 14–15
  earliest mention of, 22–23
  herbicide-resistant, 141–50
  high from, 74
  in Incan culture, 20–25
  as replacement for cocaine, 77–78
  in sixteenth-century Peru, 27–31
  taste of, 73–74
  therapeutic properties of, 21, 28,
    30–31, 66, 69, 74–76